Loving Our Neighbor

Loving Our Neighbor:

A Thoughtful Approach to Helping People in Poverty

Beth Lindsay Templeton

iUniverse, Inc.

New York Bloomington

Loving Our Neighbor
A Thoughtful Approach to Helping People in Poverty

New Revised Standard Version of the Bible, copyright 1989 by the Division of Christian Education of the National Council of the Churches of Christ in the United States of America. Used by Permission. All Rights Reserved.

Production of this book was generously underwritten by Hollingsworth Funds, Inc.

iUniverse books may be ordered through booksellers or by contacting:

iUniverse
1663 Liberty Drive
Bloomington, IN 47403
www.iuniverse.com
1-800-Authors (1-800-288-4677)

ISBN: 978-0-595-48276-4 (pbk)
ISBN: 978-0-595-71712-5 (cloth)
ISBN: 978-0-595-60362-6 (ebk)

Printed in the United States of America

For Gloria, Billy, and all the others

These twelve Jesus sent out
with the following instructions: …
Be wise as serpents and innocent as doves.
Matthew 10:5, 16b

Contents

Part Three: Poverty–The Big Picture

Acknowledgements

Thank you to all the wonderful congregations who are involved with United Ministries and who encouraged me as a minister and as a community leader.

The program participants of United Ministries are the true teachers for making wise and compassionate decisions. Each person who trusted me with his or her story, who challenged the staff about "why you won't help me," or who smiled broadly upon reaching a goal inspired me to keep working and growing. Thank you to all who shared your lives here.

The board of directors at United Ministries gave me the wonderful gift of the freedom to "preach, teach, and write." After twenty-four years as the executive director, they released me from all administrative responsibilities to do what makes "my eyes sparkle." By bringing in Keith Trout as the executive director, the board assured the ongoing success of United Ministries and encouraged me to follow my passions and dreams through developing and directing *Our Eyes Were Opened*, an outreach of United Ministries. Their support and encouragement are true blessings to me.

Debbee Gordon, Bruce Schug, Becky Bouton, Rufus Perry, Lynne Shackelford, Jean Gayle, Nancy Orders Smith, Claire Winkler, and Dot Elmore, volunteers on the Church Relations and Volunteer Committee, encouraged me from the beginning. They saw the raw material and cheered me on as I lived with the possibilities of what might come of those disconnected pieces of paper. Their belief in me and the "book" got me through some rough spots in this process. Thanks to each of you. You've truly been angels to me.

Jan Snider called me from Nashville after hearing, through the grace of God, about my workshop, "Helping Others: Servant or Sucker." In our discussions on the phone, she said, "If you've got a book inside of you, now's the time to write it." She lit the spark of possibility and cheered me on to dream beyond my little corner of the world. Thanks for your inspiration.

Steve McDonald was my longtime buddy at United Ministries. He was work partner, challenger, and friend through the seminal stages of many of the experiences which grew into *Loving Our Neighbor: A*

Thoughtful Approach to Helping People in Poverty. Because of health issues, he is no longer my foil and confidant but is still reflected in these materials.

Stephanie Brandenburg came to United Ministries at the critical time for giving birth to *Loving Our Neighbor: A Thoughtful Approach to Helping People in Poverty.* She did whatever needed to be done, held me together when the process got bogged down, and took care of those details which greatly aggravated me. What a timely gift from God. Stephanie, thanks for your friendship and your wonderful expertise. Rebecca Owens took care of many of the details of producing a manuscript. Once again, the timing of her coming to me was exquisite. Thank you, Becca, for your eagerness for the project and for your patience with me.

My family has supported me throughout the years. My sons accepted that their mom, in addition to being their mom, was passionate about United Ministries and the people the organization serves. They made sure I never took myself too seriously and always (well, almost always) assured me that we share a deep and intimate bond of love and care. In giving me daughters-in-law and grandchildren, they enriched my life beyond measure. Finally, to my husband, Jim Banks, who makes me laugh and rubs my feet, thank you for being my partner on this life journey. You are my best friend and most trusted companion.

Beth Lindsay Templeton
March 27, 2008

Introduction

Loving Our Neighbor: A Thoughtful Approach to Helping People in Poverty came about because individuals and congregations have asked repeatedly for help in knowing when and how to respond to people who ask for financial handouts. Churches, businesses, civic organizations, and school groups wanted to help but needed assistance in making wise and compassionate decisions. They asked for specific workshops. Individuals stopped me on the street with questions about how to help. Congregations asked me to preach about mission. Donors challenged me, asking why United Ministries, the nonprofit I led, did certain things in certain ways. All these questions, opportunities, and challenges led to the development of the information within this book.

Throughout my twenty-five years of working with people who need assistance as well as with people, church groups, and civic groups who want to help, I have heard comments such as:

> *"My church does not know how to deal with folks who ask for assistance. People may call on the phone, walk in during the week, or show up when we have a fellowship gathering. At times we are very lenient and help anyone who asks. At other times we are hard-nosed and help very few people. Because we really don't know what to do, we end up doing nothing."* (Patti W.)

> *"I pulled myself up. Why can't they?"*(Wade C.)

I was downtown and a guy came up to me and told me he needed to get cleaned up for his job interview tomorrow. He said, 'Just look at me. No one would hire me looking like this.' So we chatted a bit and I put him in my car and took him to a motel where he could get a good night's sleep and take a hot shower. I bought him a change of clothes and dinner. Later, I was downtown again and this same guy came up to me with the same story. I retorted that he'd told me this tale months ago when I'd helped him. I really let him have it." (James C.)

"I really want to help others. I simply don't know what to do!" (Harry H.)

You may have said similar things yourself. I know these statements come from a deep and sincere desire to help. I also know that frustration and lack of understanding negatively affect people's ability to care. *Loving Our Neighbor* will:

1. Give you an understanding of the biblical call to help.
2. Help you understand those who live in poverty.
3. Advise you of various ways you can help others.
4. Show you how to organize a direct ministry for your church.
5. Help you deepen your thoughts of the social and economic conditions that lead to poverty.

As a nonprofit executive and a minister, I have been privileged to work with people who are poor as well as with groups and individuals who want to help. I have heard numerous laments from people needing help and from people wanting to help. Those in need wonder why "no one wants to help." Those who want to help wonder why their assistance is not appreciated or does not produce good results.

Even though you want to help, in the past you may have made a bad situation worse by giving money to someone who used it to support a drug habit. You may have gotten angry at the people you wanted to help because they wouldn't behave as you thought they should. You and other potential helpers may not have known what to do.

At other times we all have come up with solutions which would work for us—people who have a strong support system and economic stability, who are privileged by skin color, age, or birth, and who are educated. Some of us cannot understand why others who don't have those same advantages cannot get their lives together. Our local paper ran an article about a young college graduate who decided to hop a train from Raleigh, North Carolina, to Charleston, South Carolina, with $25 in his pocket. Within six months, he had saved $2,500 and had a furnished apartment. This young man's story reinforced his belief that if a person would just apply himself, get a job, and stick to a plan, then life will turn out okay. [1]

Many of us need to believe that. We need to know that when we stay in school, apply ourselves at work—whether we enjoy it or not—and play by the rules, our lives will be everything we wanted. To believe otherwise is simply too scary. The newspaper story was delightful and inspiring to people who operate with these beliefs. We cannot imagine why everyone cannot do as this young man did.

The real story of the newspaper article was not that the young man made it. After all, he had a college education, he was white and good looking, and he understood middle-class ways of thinking and acting. He did not come from poverty where the rules of the middle class are unknown. Reading between the lines of the news story, his family was stable, he knew how to speak in formal, educated English, and no one in his immediate family was an addict or mentally unstable. He could interact with employers because he intuitively understood their language, their rules, and their values. Charleston, the community of his experiment, had an adequate public transportation system. He had no medical emergency. Of course, he was able to succeed.

The real story was that many of us believe that his story can be true for anyone in our country. After all, we are a bootstrap nation. We believe that we create our own destinies. We are masters of our fate. We can be whoever and whatever we choose to be.

Tell that to someone who grew up in a family where violence was a routine occurrence. Every night a child's sleep was disturbed by screaming and the noises of fighting and throwing things. Every day that same child could not concentrate in school because of sleep deprivation and so fell farther and farther behind. Tell it to someone who had an undiagnosed learning disability, dropped out of school, and was limited to working three part-time jobs in order to care for the family. Tell it to someone who worked for years in the same position, only to discover she was no longer employable when the plant closed. Tell it to someone whose employer could not afford to provide health care and the heart attack meant loss of everything material. Tell it to the young person of color who is suspect because his name sounds "foreign."

Many of us want to blame people who live in poverty for creating their situation. It protects our own sense of security. Until we realize that we have been enriched by situations, experiences, and systems of privilege that are not of our own making, we will continue to see with only limited vision and understanding the problems of our disadvantaged neighbors. We will not grasp the depth of the challenges or the height of the obstacles faced by people who live in poverty.

Because I had been given the opportunity to know deeply people who live in poverty, I realized I could help others who did not have that privilege to understand what my United Ministries program participant friends were facing and struggling with. Because my first career was as a teacher, I could develop workshops, seminars, and simulations which helped people open their eyes. Because I am a minister and believe that people of faith are called to reach out to others and to be partners with the Holy God in creating communities of wholeness and peace, I could articulate my understandings from the perspective of faith. Because I led a human services nonprofit for twenty-four years, and because we tried a lot of approaches that did not produce the results we wanted, I could speak with authority about what worked and what didn't.

Through the years I was invited to meet with church groups who wanted to help but knew they lacked understanding. I watched United Ministries' program participants respond to our program staff's trial-and-error efforts as we all learned how to provide life-changing opportunities. I discovered a significant disconnect between what people wanted to do for others and what actually resulted. People who wanted to help needed insight into issues of poverty so they could reach out with wisdom and empathy. I realized I could help people who had power, money, and a desire to care and to understand more about people who live in poverty. I could help people with resources feel the challenges poverty creates, challenges far different from their own. I knew people wanted to know what kinds of questions to ask and which to avoid. I could help them learn to see the world with eyes opened beyond their own limited experiences. I knew people wanted to develop real relationships with people in need and to do more than simply write a check. I knew they wanted to feel good about helping others, and they wanted their help to build strength in the lives of the people to whom they reached out.

With this desire to increase understanding, I began to preach, teach, and write from the experience I had gained from listening to the program participants of United Ministries. *Loving Our Neighbor: A Thoughtful Approach to Helping People in Poverty* grew out of all the conversations, setbacks, and successes of the last quarter century. People who received services at United Ministries as well as those who participated in my workshops and seminars in the community challenged me. They, along with United Ministries' board, volunteers, and staff, trusted me with deep questions. Members of congregations who listened to my sermons or participated in a Bible study, Sunday school class, or retreat guided me to new levels of understanding. Groups large and small gave me the platform to try to articulate and share all I was learning.

I had already developed handouts for use in our community. The next logical step was to write *Loving Our Neighbor: A Thoughtful Approach to Helping People in Poverty*.

The book is intentionally designed to be user friendly. It can be read cover to cover. It can be used over several sessions in a church school class, adult discussion group, or service committee conversation. Questions, worksheets, and exercises at the end of each chapter help expand your learning opportunities. You may focus on one specific section or skip around. Each chapter and each section are written to stand alone, if desired.

I acknowledge that the book is written from a Christian perspective because I am a Presbyterian U.S.A. minister. I hope that readers from other faith traditions or from none will find the materials helpful with minor "translations" on their part.

Part One: The Biblical Call to Love Our Neighbor grew out of sermons which challenged people of faith to take the scriptures very seriously and to live their lives in ways that exhibited their faith through caring and loving. By looking at familiar scripture passages—the Beatitudes; the commandment to love God, neighbor, and self; Jesus as the way, truth, and life; and doing justice, loving mercy, and walking with God—we have guidance for why people of faith reach out to others.

Part Two: A Thoughtful Approach to Deciding How, When, and Whom to Help addresses ways to reach out to others without feeling as if you've been conned; different ways in which congregations help others; how to set up a direct aid ministry; and how to make decisions for using a congregation's benevolence dollars.

Part Three: Poverty—The Big Picture helps deepen our understanding of issues of poverty so we can branch out in our responses to need.

Loving Our Neighbor: A Thoughtful Approach to Helping People in Poverty is an opportunity to share with you the lessons I have learned through the years. For example, I learned that in our efforts to be welcoming and hospitable with homeless people, we were inadvertently helping them to be homeless. We washed some people's clothes for six years! We allowed people to "hang out" with no questions asked. We eventually learned that the word *no* is sometimes the most caring word we can say. Hopefully you will be challenged to reach out to others with wisdom and compassion without making so many of the mistakes I did.

Part One:

The Biblical Call to Love Our Neighbor

Chapter One

The Beatitudes as a Guide for Loving Our Neighbor
Matthew 5:1–12

WHEN I FIRST LEARNED about the Beatitudes, I thought they were about me and my faith development. I was to be meek and peace loving. Mourning was to be welcomed. As I matured both professionally and in my faith journey, I realized that they could also be teaching how I might love my neighbor as myself. They point us to the reality that when we share in the life of someone who is struggling and witness that person overcoming tremendous obstacles, we celebrate.

I met Gloria in the early 1990s. She was an addict and a prostitute. Her drug of choice was alcohol. Her addiction was so intense that she had to get up in the night to drink to maintain the alcohol level in her body. She actually believed she was called by God to be a prostitute. When I asked her how she figured that, she said, "I got a legitimate job as a dishwasher. One day I was leaning over the sink washing dishes, and the boss man came up behind me. He leaned into me and whispered that I didn't have to keep scrubbing those pots. I could come into his office and take care of him. I decided that even though I had tried to do right, I was still treated as a prostitute. I figured that must be what God wanted me to do."

Eventually Gloria was, as she reports it, delivered by God from her addiction. She left prostitution and got a job in a franchise restaurant.

After two years there, she was earning less than $7.00 an hour with no benefits. She was hurt on the job, but the company refused to file worker's compensation for her. Eventually by using three different attorneys, Gloria was able to get what was rightfully hers. By then the damage in her back was so severe that she required several operations and a hip replacement. Today Gloria is a graduate of a culinary school and is completing her GED.

Working with Gloria gives me deep and abiding joy–the kind of joy spoken of in the Beatitudes. They show us what we can be; but just as with Gloria's journey, the lessons found in the Beatitudes require work and lots of support, guidance, nurture, and compassion from others and from God. Many read the Beatitudes as a soothing word from God. They certainly can be read that way. However, the Beatitudes can challenge us in the short term and yet leave us with permanent joy for the long term.

Maybe if we talk about "permanent joy" first, the rest will be easier for us to hear. Let's start with the word which is often translated as "blessed." The Greek word is *makarios*. Some translate this particular word as "fortunate," "lucky," "happy," or "congratulations." These don't quite capture the full intent of *makarios*. The Greek word describes a kind of joy which is permanent, which holds a deep secret. I relate *makarios* to the joy I felt the month before my fiancé and I shared with anyone else that we were going to get married. That secret was special. *Makarios* is like the joy you have when, years after the fact, you discover that your words spoken long ago were the catalyst for another to make significant changes in his or her life. *Makarios* is the kind of joy which is deep and abiding. It is not dependent on what is going on around us. It is within us—a gift from God. It is blessing in the fullest sense of the word. *Makarios* is what Gloria shines with when I see her in her chef's hat because she knows that I know the story of her journey.

Jesus describes different ways in which people experience this kind of permanent joy. He talks about being in the kingdom of God (or of heaven). This is about living in a world where God is ruler, where God sets the rules, where God defines the relationships, where God provides for all, and where God loves us into being the good creation God intended. Jesus says that people who live in permanent joy are comforted. They inherit the earth. In other words, they will live in the kingdom of God. People with permanent joy are filled and receive mercy. Don't we all want this? Don't we all yearn for the experience of everyone laughing and dancing and living with our Holy God in the midst of us all, enjoying every minute with us?

The Beatitudes give us a step-by-step approach to living in God's grace and living through caring for others. Jesus teaches us about the permanent joy we experience when we share life with God and the Glorias of this world.

Matthew 5:3 – "Blessed [*makarios*/ permanently joyful] are the poor in spirit, for theirs is the kingdom of heaven."

We may think that "poor in spirit" describes people who are depressed or lethargic. Some people see "poor in spirit" as a psychological term. To understand Jesus' meaning of "poor in spirit," we need to remember that he was speaking Aramaic which has its roots in Hebrew. Deuteronomy 8:11–20 helps capture the Hebrew sense of "poor in spirit." Those verses begin with: "Take care that you do not forget the LORD your God, by failing to keep his commandments, his ordinances, and his statutes, which I am commanding you today." The passage tells of all the things God had done for the people in leading them out of Egypt. Then it says, "When you have eaten your fill and have built fine houses and live in them ... and your silver and gold is multiplied, ... then do not exalt yourself, forgetting the LORD your God ... But remember the LORD your God, for it is he who gives you power to get wealth" (verses 12–14, 18). Therefore, a person who is poor in spirit is not someone who is poor economically or who chooses to be poor for religious reasons. It is not someone who is depressed. Rather "poor in spirit" refers to those people who are dependent not on their own accomplishments and their own accumulation for security but are dependent on God's grace. "Poor in spirit" refers to those who realize that material things mean nothing. God means everything.

Gloria regularly acknowledges that she is who she is now because God and certain people care about her. She feels rich not because of material possessions but because of God's goodness in her life. One of the realities I have witnessed among people with whom I work is the deep and abiding thankfulness they articulate to Jesus—no matter what is going on in their lives. They may be down to their last dollar, but they will share that dollar with someone who is needier than they. The staff of United Ministries may have to tell them that we cannot help again because we have already paid a bill for them, and they will still say, "Thank you, Jesus." They may tell of tragedy heaped on tragedy and still acknowledge their dependence on God rather than on material things.

Being poor in spirit is the first major stomp on our toes. Can we honestly claim that things mean nothing to us? How much time and energy do we spend fretting about what we do have? Does it need repair? Where will I put it? Is it the look that I am after? We fret about what we don't have. "I *need* another … whatever." "Every other church has a van, a gym, a state-of-the-art nursery … whatever. *We need one too!*" We live and act sometimes as if things mean everything and God means nothing. It is a myth that possessing more and more things will make us happy.

This first Beatitude points us to the fact that we are totally dependent on God. And when we claim and live that reality, we have permanent joy.

Matthew 5:4 – "Blessed [*makarios/* permanently joyful] are those who mourn, for they will be comforted."

We usually think that "mourn" refers to those who are grieving over the loss of a loved one. Once again we need to look at the Old Testament for the sense of Jesus' teaching. In Isaiah 61:1–4, we read about the oppressed, the brokenhearted, the captives, and the prisoners. Mourning in this passage refers to those who mourn the devastation of Israel. They mourn the Israelites' disobedience, which brought about their captivity. When we look beyond ourselves, we can mourn the conditions facing people who are oppressed, brokenhearted, captive, or prisoners. They live in our community. We can mourn their situations.

With the first Beatitude, we acknowledge that all we are and ever will be is of God. With the second, we look beyond ourselves and see all the other people. We can mourn what is happening to them. We mourn that Gloria felt she had no options as a young woman other than to work as a prostitute and use drugs to get through the day. We mourn the lack of food and medical care that some of our neighbors experience. We mourn that some in our communities must live in houses that would not be fit for our dogs. We mourn that people cannot earn enough to provide adequately for their families, even though they are working sixty or more hours a week. We mourn a world where violence is the primary tool for solving conflicts and problems. We mourn the devastation from hurricanes or earthquakes. We mourn how we become detached from others as we hunker down in our own little worlds. We mourn our own apathy.

When we mourn, others can see us in our full humanity. People can relate to us. When others mourn, we can empathize with them and begin to understand some of their pain. Any of us who have gone through some kind of personal devastation know that, all of a sudden, people feel more comfortable in talking with us about their own problems because they realize that we understand. We have walked their path. We have experienced some of their struggle.

When we are open to the vulnerability of the world, we will experience permanent joy.

Matthew 5:5 – "Blessed [*makarios/* permanently joyful] are the meek, for they will inherit the earth."

Meek does not mean being a doormat. Who wants to be that? Because we are the recipients of God's love and grace, even though we do not deserve those gifts, we too can be loving and gracious to others. Aristotle describes meekness as that center point between too much anger and too little anger. When we think of being meek, we can think of the *power of love* or of what Gandhi called *soul force*. In our meekness, we know that we are not God. We do not have to dominate the world. If we need a human image of meekness, we can think of Rosa Parks, a seamstress in Montgomery, Alabama, who in 1955 refused to give up her seat on a bus and quietly, yet forcefully, claimed her uniqueness as a daughter of God. She wasn't trying to begin a movement. Parks was simply wanting to get home at the end of a tiring day of work.

Being meek means that when we meet someone who is seeking our assistance, in whatever form, we can be kind and gracious. With good reason we may not choose to honor their request, but we can honor their humanity and worthiness as a child of God. When someone approaches us on the street asking for a handout, we can be loving as we say, "I will not give you money now, but I have information about where you can go for long-term help so that you do not have to be on the street asking folks like me for money." We can point them to temporary shelters, case management services, addiction treatment centers, or mental health clinics. We can engage them in love without giving them money, which might deliver them to death through drugs. We encounter them as people in need of more or different kinds of help than we have to offer.

When we choose to be in relationships with women such as Gloria, we choose to honor the gifts she exhibits. We acknowledge that we do not know what it feels like to live in her skin, to have experienced the conditions of her life, or to know the best solutions for next steps. We know we care and that we're willing to walk alongside her, learning from her as she learns from us.

Matthew 5:6 – "Blessed [*makarios*/ permanently joyful] are those who hunger and thirst for righteousness, for they will be filled."

This teaching has to do with a yearning for social justice—for righteousness. This is not simply a nice thought: "Wouldn't it be nice if we built a Habitat house, if we opened a medical clinic, if we had a letter-writing campaign to increase funding for child care." All these things *are* important. However, this verse speaks of hungering and thirsting.

Hungering is more than needing an afternoon snack to get us through to dinnertime. Hungering is about that feeling one gets when the money runs out before the month runs out, and there is no food in the house. Hungering is about having a bloated belly and bugged-out eyes because you have not had a square meal in weeks. Do we have that kind of yearning for social justice? Do we thirst like someone stranded in the desert thirsts for water? Do we thirst that way for a world where everyone can meet his or her needs and where all can reach the full potential God created in them? Do we have that gut kind of yearning for righteousness?

When we learn a pupil in our own child's class is hurting in some way, do we champion for that child as we would for our own? Do we act on our feelings of disgust when we learn of injustices, or do we simply say, "That's awful," and forget about it the next day? Do we really hunger for the well-being of everyone in our own community?

I told you these verses were challenging. However, when we are engaged in God's world with the Beatitudes' depth of love and concern, we experience permanent joy, according to Jesus.

Matthew 5:7 – "Blessed [*makarios/* permanently joyful] are the merciful, for they will receive mercy."

Are you beginning to see a pattern here? When we are poor in spirit, we acknowledge our total dependence on God. We mourn as we see the pain and devastation in the world. In meekness we realize we have all and none of the solutions for others. With intense yearning, we hunger for healing in the world. And then we offer mercy, God's steadfast loving-kindness, that reaches out to everyone, deserving and undeserving.

Mercy is not an attitude: "Oh, I feel compassion for you." No, mercy is action. We put ourselves in the other's place to try to see, taste, touch, hear, and smell the world as he or she does. We try to see life as Gloria might see it.

Mercy tempers our sense of righteousness. Without mercy we may try to deal with our hunger and thirst for righteousness by being ruthless, aggressive, or violent. Being merciful reminds us that the kingdom of God is in God's hands, not ours. We can admit that God has indeed been merciful with us, even when we did not deserve it. As we live in God's grace, we can offer that same kind of freedom, accountability, and love to another of God's beloved children. We can enjoy Gloria's company even when we do not approve of her choices. We can love her into accountability for her actions. As she moves into the new life which is ahead for her, she can experience freedom which she never knew existed when she was trapped in abuse, fear, and poor self-image.

Sometimes people have told me that they do not want to reach out to others. They don't want to help people who made bad choices which led to their current condition. Yes, people do make bad choices.

Don't we all? Mercy says that maybe, just maybe, we can reach out yet one more time, offer an alternative to previous bad decisions, and love with both wisdom and compassion so a person can grow into a healthier way of living.

Matthew 5:8 – "Blessed [*makarios*/ permanently joyful] are the pure in heart, for they will see God."

Being pure in heart follows naturally when we no longer yearn for things, when we are able to mourn, when we hunger for what is right because we are full of mercy, and see others as beloved people of God. Psalm 24:3–4 states, "Who shall ascend the hill of the Lord? … Those who have clean hands and pure hearts, who do not lift up their souls to what is false, and do not swear deceitfully." The pure in heart, according to the psalmist, are not only people who are innocent of moral failures but who are also free of evil intentions. The Hebrews believed the heart to be the seat of will, so being pure in heart meant simply having purity of will.

When conversing with dedicated people of faith who ask about the wisdom of giving money to people who come up to them on the street asking for a handout, I ask them why they give money. With reluctance, they often acknowledge they give because they want the person to go away, they are afraid, or they feel guilty. They admit that their response is not in the manner which Jesus teaches. They are acting not with a pure heart but rather from an impulse that is guarded and protected.

Matthew 5:9 – "Blessed [*makarios*/ permanently joyful] are the peacemakers, for they will be called children of God."

We now know we are dependent on God. We see the pain in the world around us. We yearn for a world where everyone enjoys the full knowledge and benefit of God's love. We are merciful toward those with whom we disagree or who frustrate us or who challenge us in a variety of ways. Now what?

Now we do something about all that. We make peace. We don't *keep* peace. We make it. We do that hard work of reconciling hostile individuals or situations. We strive to return good for evil and to love those we do not like. We painstakingly build bridges when every fiber of our being would rather build walls.

Peacemaking is hard work. It is ten times, a thousand times, incalculably harder than keeping peace. Keeping peace often allows secrets to continue wreaking their havoc in their dark hiddenness. Keeping peace means that people "play nice" to each other's face and knife each other in the back through phone calls or parking-lot meetings or e-mail messages or letter campaigns. Yes, making peace is harder. When we are peacemakers, we have permanent, deep, and abiding joy—according to Jesus.

We are tempted to *keep* peace by remaining silent when someone tells an offensive joke about people of a certain ethnic group, skin color, sexual preference, gender, age, or religious affiliation. We can *make* peace when we confront the stereotype being expressed, when we say that we do not think the joke is funny and tell why, or when we stand up to the rest of the group who are laughing out of ignorance, prejudice, or discomfort.

We keep peace when we sweep Gloria and her friends out of our communities so that we will not have to deal with "those women." We make peace when we provide opportunities for them to change their lives in healthy, life-nurturing ways. We make peace when Gloria finds positive ways to leave prostitution, kicks her addiction, and is trained to be the catering chef she has always wanted to be.

Matthew 5:10–11 – "Blessed [*makarios*/ permanently joyful] are those who are persecuted for righteousness' sake, for theirs is the kingdom of heaven. Blessed are you when people revile you and persecute you and utter all kinds of evil against you falsely on my account."

People who love as God loves, who are dependent on God, who allow the woes of the world to penetrate their innermost being, and then choose to do something about it ... those people are likely to experience discord, antagonism, hatred, ostracism, and, yes, even death. Look what happened to Jesus. Jesus is not telling us to do anything he did not do.

Gandhi was persecuted when he stood up for his people in India to be treated fairly as valuable human beings. Martin Luther King Jr.

was assassinated when he stood up against racism and war. Nelson Mandela served decades of prison time for standing up against apartheid in South Africa. When people worked with Gloria to help her get a job and overcome her addictions, others in the community challenged her advocates by saying, "No way. She's just a hooker. Nothing good will come of this! Who do you think you are?" Ordinary people who stand up for fair housing, public transportation, health care for all, and equitable wages and join the struggle against societal ills are labeled with "crazy," "nuts," "extremist," "anti-Christian," and lots of other negative epithets. Standing up for what is right and just is not easy but does offer a state called *makarios*, permanently joyful, according to Jesus.

When we take our faith seriously, when we choose to let our faith influence and permeate every fiber, impulse, and act, of course, we will be compelled at times to say unpopular things, to take unpopular stands, or to speak God's truth as we understand it to people who love living with lies. Jesus tells us that those actions that scare us are the very actions of deep, abiding, permanent joy.

These teachings of Jesus simply do not make sense in our rational ways of thinking in the twenty-first century. These Beatitudes turn everything upside down. Our world says to get what we can. If others are poor, that's not our fault. We work hard, and since they are poor, they must not work. Our world says to pay attention to me and mine. We can ignore people who are poor or needy. The needs of others are not our concerns. Our world says to let the chips fall where they may, to ignore others because they get what they deserve, to live insulated lives behind gates, and to get others before they do unto you. These are the teachings of our world.

Jesus sits and teaches us just the opposite. Jesus tells us that living in his way, walking his path, following him as Lord and Savior, and being his disciple is where we discover permanent joy. When we reach out, when we care, when we work for the good of others, when we live as Jesus challenges us to live, we experience the reality of *makarios*: deep, abiding, and permanent joy. Do we dare believe that?

Questions to Consider

1. Do you agree or disagree with this way of considering the Beatitudes? Why?

2. How does this treatment of the Beatitudes affect how you think about people who are poor?

3. How do the Beatitudes affect what you think a faithful follower of Christ is and does?

4. Do the Beatitudes issue a call to action for you personally? If so, what is the call?

5. Having looked at the Beatitudes now, you will never be the same again. Do you agree or disagree? So what?

Prayer

God of all goodness, we thank you for instilling your love and compassion in people in our community. The caring of a lot of people is remarkable. And yet, Gracious God, we ask that you nudge us to see the lives and conditions of people we have not yet seen, to hear the words of pain and frustration and defeat that we have not yet heard, and to touch the realities of neighbors where we have not yet wanted to be. We thank you for your love and compassion. We ask for more.

God, our Source and our End, we thank you that you have given us minds and hearts to make a difference in our community. And yet, Holy One, we ask that you show us how feeble our attempts are in light of all that we have the power and ability to do. Urge us with dissatisfaction in the disparities in our community. Throw us off balance when we take pride in the things that we do and neglect the needs that stare us in our faces. Remove the crusts from our hearts so we can feel with those who are vulnerable in our community. We thank you for our dedicated minds and hearts. We ask for more.

God, our Guide and Inspiration, we thank you for the leadership that you have placed in our community. We ask that you fill with wisdom the men and women who show us the way. Temper their drive with compassion, their control with awareness, and their power with steadfast love. Source of all life, fill them with a yearning to use their gifts and graces for the benefit of all our citizens even when their friends desire otherwise. We thank you for our leaders and ask even more for them.

In love and service, we pray. Amen.

Chapter Two

Loving Totally

Mark 12:28–34

"Which commandment is the first of all?" Jesus answered, "The
first is, 'Hear, O Israel: the Lord our God, the Lord is one; you
shall love the Lord your God with all your heart, and with all
your soul, and with all your mind, and with all your strength.'
The second is this, 'You shall love your neighbor as yourself.'
There is no other commandment greater than these."
(Mark 12: 28b–31)

THOSE OF US WHO have been followers of Jesus' way for a long time
may find these commandments quoted by Jesus very familiar…
maybe too familiar. If we have been instructed in the church, we *know*
we are to love God with all our heart, soul, mind, and strength and
to love our neighbor as ourselves. We have heard this all our lives.
Suppose, though, just suppose that we have never heard this teaching.
Is it possible for us to try to hear it as something brand new? Can we
imagine that we have just come to visit a church? We are exploring
that small yearning in our heart to learn more about this connection
with God.

We, as visitors and searchers, sit in our seats and look around.
We see beautiful architecture or artistic banners and listen to
inspirational music. And then a minister stands up and reads: "The

first [commandment] is 'Hear, O Israel: the Lord our God, the Lord is one ...'" Now we are being pulled into the wonder of God's Word.

These words, "The Lord our God, the Lord is one," are powerful beyond measure. These words have been said every morning and every evening by people who are Jewish for more than 2,200 years (Deuteronomy 6:4–5). Every morning and every evening! Wow. Jesus repeated these words himself as a child, as a youth, as a young man, and as a teacher. With these words, he was connecting with the religious leaders who were trying to trick him into saying something which would get him into *big* trouble. When Jesus repeated, "Hear, O Israel ...," which is called the Shema, he was affirming two things: one, that he was a Jew, just like the people with whom he was talking, and two, that he believed and proclaimed there was only one God.

Now this was an important affirmation in a culture where many gods were worshiped. The Romans who were occupying Palestine had a whole pantheon of gods. Today this Shema is something we Christians might consider taking to heart. What if we affirmed morning and evening that we believed in the one God? If we did so, would we be less likely to worship all the things which occupy our time ... all the stuff we worry about acquiring, keeping, storing, getting rid of? If daily we claimed one God, would we focus more on the Holy One and less on winning at all costs at work, in the church, or at home? Would we be more willing to look at the ways we push God out of the center of our lives and how we replace that God hole in our hearts with junk thoughts, junk ambitions, junk relationships, and junk things?

So Jesus begins by amplifying the Shema. He describes how we are to love this one God. He says, "You shall love the Lord your God with all your heart, and with all your soul, and with all your mind, and with all your strength." This is a very complete way of loving: heart, soul, mind, and strength.

Biblical love is not based on feeling, on the sentiments of Valentine cards, or the flutter of the heart when in the presence of someone. Biblical love is commitment to another, no matter how good or bad, no matter how endearing or obnoxious. Biblical love is action, not feeling, a way of choosing rather than a way of reacting. When we love God, we love because we *choose* to love, not because we are feeling close or warm or fuzzy. Certainly there are times when we feel overwhelmed by our good and gracious God. There are other times, though, when our *decision* to follow Christ's way is the only sense we have of being connected to the Source of our life. We discover that at times we must remind ourselves that we have committed our lives to being faithful and loving—because we certainly don't feel that way!

Love is a need of life itself. Love is that sense of connectedness when the "is-ness" of one person recognizes the "is-ness" of another person. In the holy sense, then, love of God addresses our need for an intimate relationship with the creator of the vastness beyond ourselves, to connect with the One who cares for us more deeply and more completely than any human we know, and to fulfill our deep search for meaning and completeness beyond our wildest imagination. Love of God is committing to the One who yearns to be engaged with us and then experiencing all the joy and wonder that communion entails.

So to love in that way, we commit with our whole being. In the Hebrew way of thinking, the heart is the center of will. To love with our *heart* is to choose to love, to address the need of being connected with God who is greater than we can dream and who is as close as our own breath. We choose to love God in order to act on our passion for God's guidance, grace, truth, and wisdom. We choose to love. Now choosing is not something we do once, and it is done forever. We sometimes must choose daily or every hour because there will be plenty of opportunities for us to choose to place our allegiance elsewhere. Other enticements for worship and adoration will come to us regularly. Television commercials entice us to adore bathroom cleaners or financial planners or government policies. We are bombarded with other calls for our allegiances and priorities. Choosing to love God is a daily responsibility and joy.

We commit with our *soul*. What in the world do we mean by that? Theologians throughout the centuries have discussed and argued about what the soul is, when it is created, and where it is located. For our purposes, we can think of soul as our life force, our energy, or our spirit. The soul is where our enthusiasm resides, where our hope lives, and where our joy bubbles. We can love God with our laughter, our tears, our visions, and our frustrations. We can love God with our anger, our commitments, our courage, and our fears. We can love God with our soul.

We commit to God with our *mind*. We actually think about holy things. We question. We challenge. We study. We read. We discuss. We dialogue. We do not pronounce that we know all, that we have the final, last word, or that we have inner knowledge which gives us the power to rule the world, our community, our church, or our family. We love God with our mind, always seeking to learn more about what it means to be a faithful person, what it means to be a disciple of Jesus, or what it means to follow in Jesus' footsteps. In loving God with our mind, we acknowledge that we may have a bit of the truth; someone else might have another bit; and someone else has yet another bit. Together we will get closer to the truth, but we will never arrive at the whole truth about our loving God.

Job thought he knew the right and wrong ways of the world until God responded with "Do you give the horse its might? Do you clothe its neck with mane?"(Job 39:19). After being given many other examples of how God's knowledge and ways are vaster than we can ever conceive, Job answered, "I know that you can do all things, and that no purpose of yours can be thwarted ... I have uttered what I did not understand, things too wonderful for me, which I did not know" (Job 42:2–3). Therefore, we journey with God through committing our mind to this Holy One.

We commit to God with our *strength*. We love God with our physical self. We care for our body as a holy vessel so that our hands can serve God. We can use our feet in God's service. We can use our ears, our eyes, and our mouth to serve.

Someone who is just exploring faith and hearing all this for the first time might say, "That all sounds very good, but how can I love God when I cannot see God?" That's actually a very good question.

In Jesus' life and ministry, he demonstrated how we can show our love for God. The most famous passage for how that happens is Matthew 25:31–46 when Jesus says (verses 35–36, 40) that when we feed hungry people, we feed *him*. When we clothe naked people, we clothe *him*. When we give a thirsty person something to drink, we quench *his* thirst.

So how do we demonstrate to ourselves and to the world that we truly love God with our heart, soul, mind, and strength? We love our neighbors. We love the people who need our love. We love people who hurt in all manner of ways—emotionally, physically, spiritually, or economically. This is not always easy, is it? We can easily love those people who are most like us, who think like we do, who value what we value, or who are enjoyable to be with. We find it harder to love people who make us angry, threaten us, or degrade what we find most important. We *really* find it hard to love people who stink, are lazy, make our lives difficult, or make us feel small.

Many churches have signs out front that say, "All are welcome." When a church displays this greeting, the members want to be hospitable. They really believe that anyone can come into their fellowship and experience the warmth and support they each receive there for themselves. Their sense of welcome is sincerely grounded in their belief in Christ's invitation to come to him.

However, if Clarence entered, a man who had not bathed in days and who was babbling nonsense, would the members truly welcome him? Love is action, not feeling. Would *you* be able to welcome Clarence? Would you be able to invite him to sit with you? Would you offer him your hand when he looks so nasty? When you decide to love him, will you reach out to him no matter what? Might you take him to a shower facility after the service? Loving him means being willing to be his friend or advocate. Loving him means patting his shoulder or holding his hand … if that will comfort him. Loving him means choosing to love … not feeling warm, loving feelings.

There is a great deal in the Bible about loving our neighbor. The Samaritan traveler helped the victim of robbery alongside the road even though he could just as easily have ignored that person. Jesus reached out repeatedly to people who were blind, to women with long-term illnesses, to those who needed a good meal, and to lepers who were despised by society. Jesus showed us over and over how to love our neighbor. We too have neighbors who are despised because of illness (mental or physical), sexual orientation, color of skin, quality of speech, accent, or general attitude. We know *what* we as faithful people are called to do. Sometimes we just have trouble doing it. Sometimes we do not *will* to actively care about the welfare of others.

But Jesus taught us that in caring for others, we care for him. He even gave us a measuring rod for how to think about loving our neighbors. He said to love them as we love ourselves. This was not original with Jesus. He was quoting Leviticus 19:18, which says, "You shall not take vengeance or bear a grudge against any of your people, but you shall love your neighbor as yourself: I am the LORD."

Jesus reminded his followers that loving neighbors means that we take their needs as seriously as we do our own. If we believe that we should be listened to, then we listen to others. If we believe that we deserve respect, then we respect others—as hard as that might be. If we get a new coat, do we get a new coat for our neighbor who might be homeless, or do we provide a used one which might be too big? If we value decent, affordable homes for our families, can we value decent, affordable homes for other people as well and then work to make them a reality? This loving our neighbor as ourselves gets played out in many different ways. Each of us can meditate on the areas in our lives in which we are not loving ourselves and certainly not loving our neighbors as ourselves.

Connie Rouse wrote a beautiful true story entitled "The Homecoming Triumph." [2] She told of Mary, a wonderful young woman, who was kind and bubbly. However, her learning disabilities required her to attend special classes. Because other students made fun of pupils in the special class and because the school wanted to teach tolerance, the staff developed a mentor program which matched students without learning disabilities with those who found learning difficult. John, star of the football team, president of the student body, and an excellent student, was Mary's mentor. To help Mary fulfill a wish, he decided to ask her to be his escort for the homecoming court. Mary's parents did not trust John's generous invitation at first. They were afraid that the other students would not allow a person they labeled as "retarded" to win. John asked his friends to help him campaign for Mary. All the girls in the homecoming court, of course, hoped they would be crowned homecoming queen. No one expected what happened. The other girls asked their fellow students to vote for Mary rather than for them because they knew the courage it took for Mary to run, and they wanted her to win.

My friend wrote of this student body: "Mary may have won the crown that night but every student at that school was a winner. They had been given the gift of humility and kindness. They had learned to let go of their own ambitions and prejudices. The students experienced the triumph of the human spirit. They had come to understand that we are our brother's and sister's keepers. They learned that we are all a part of God's creating and that if we work together and trust in God, then we can make the world a better place." This is loving the Lord, our God, with all our heart, soul, mind, and strength and our neighbor as ourself.

There is one final point in this passage. The religious authority who was questioning Jesus acknowledged that commitment to the one Lord, to our neighbor, and to ourselves was better than all the ritual and religious functions which we value. The scribe said,

> "You are right, Teacher; you have truly said that
> '[God] is one, and besides [the Lord] there is no
> other'; and 'to love [God] with all the heart, and
> with all the understanding, and with all the strength,'
> and 'to love one's neighbor as oneself,'—this is much
> more important than all whole burnt offerings and
> sacrifices."
> (Mark 12:32–33)

Sometimes we get overly tied to our orders of worship, to the kinds of music allowed in worship, to the times we worship, to the style of dress we wear to worship, or to the colors used in the sanctuary. This scribe pointed out to Jesus that these kinds of things are not nearly as important as our love of God, neighbor, and self. And what did Jesus say? "You are not far from the kingdom of God" (Mark 12:34).

We are charged to focus on drawing close to the kingdom of God by committing to the one Lord and loving our Holy God with all our heart, our soul, our mind, and our strength—and by loving our neighbor as ourselves. As we live out these two commandments with God's help, we will experience the fullness of being a follower of our Lord, Jesus Christ.

Questions to Consider

1. How would using the Shema affect your daily interactions with your neighbor?

2. If today was the first time you heard about loving God, your neighbor, and yourself as a way to be faithful, how would you react? Is this good news? Bad news? News that doesn't change a thing?

3. Would someone who knew you well say that you love God more than your neighbor? Your neighbor more than God? Yourself more than God? Yourself more than your neighbor?

4. How does your congregation demonstrate that it follows these two commandments?

5. Does this passage call you to action?

6. Having looked at these commandments, you will never be the same again. Do you agree or disagree? Why?

Prayer

Most loving God, we come to you with mixed motives. We ask that you guide us to care for and help people who are in need. We confess that we want to help without any inconvenience or sacrifice on our part. We want all people to live in harmony and love but not if it means we have to give a little on our closely held beliefs and concepts. We yearn for every person in our community to have opportunity to become self-reliant. However, we prefer that their self-reliance come with no accommodation on our part.

Holy One for Peace, help us to see joy in service where before we saw inconvenience. Give us openness to hear another's portion of the truth that we do not have because our reality is incomplete, too. Lead us to flexibility so that we can bend to another's needs. Give us loving hearts and willing minds to work and live and play so that all may know your grace.

Amen.

Chapter Three

Walking the Way?

John 14

Jesus said to [Thomas], "I am the way, and the truth, and the life. No one comes to the Father except through me." (John 14:6)

A CHILDREN'S SUNDAY SCHOOL SONG says, "Jesus loves me, this I know. For the Bible tells me so." [3] A preeminent theologian of the twentieth century, Karl Barth, is reported to have summed up his basic beliefs using these words: "Jesus loves me." Jesus loves us. What more do we need?

Dr. Shirley Guthrie, in his book, *Always Being Reformed, Faith for a Fragmented World* reminds us:

> God's love [was/is] not just for Christians but for all
> humanity … [Jesus] came not to give his followers
> everything they wanted to be happy, successful,
> and secure now and forever, but to announce and
> usher in the worldwide reign of God's justice and
> compassion for *everyone*. He was the friend not just
> of law-abiding, God-fearing insiders, but of sinful,
> unbelieving, or different-believing outsiders. He
> believed that caring for suffering and needy human
> beings was more important than conformity to the
> moral and theological requirements of religious

orthodoxy. He came not to condemn, defeat, and
lord it over those who rejected him but to give his
life for them, to restore to them their own true
humanity and to reconcile them to God and their
fellow human beings. And God raised *him* from the
dead and made *him* to be the crucified and risen Lord
over all principalities and authorities everywhere ...
[e]ven where he is not yet known, acknowledged, and
served; even before Christians get there to tell others
about him. [4]

The Presbyterian Church U.S.A. was able to affirm:

The limits of salvation, whatever they may be, are
known only to God. Three truths above all are
certain. God is a holy God who is not to be trifled
with. No one will be saved except by grace alone.
And no judge could possibly be more gracious than
our Lord and Savior, Jesus Christ. [5]

A Hindu scholar reminded those of us who are Christian that
following Jesus is not a matter of affirming a specific set of beliefs but
is a way of being transformed and brought into a new reality beyond
our wildest imaginings when he said,

This verse (John 14:6) is absolutely true ... Jesus is
the only way. And that way ... of dying to an old way
of living and being born into a new way of being ...
is known to all the religions of the world. [6]

So, having heard all that, who *is* this Jesus for us? Each of us
probably has a different way of talking about who Jesus is in our life.
Some of us always pray to Jesus, not the Father and not the Spirit.
Some of us talk with Jesus daily, if not constantly, as if he were right
beside us.

Jesus is God, fully, and Jesus is human, fully. Jesus as both human
and divine is a concept we cannot get our minds around. There have

been arguments about Jesus' divinity and humanity throughout the centuries. We simply choose which pieces of the picture of Jesus we can deal with at a particular moment. Hopefully as we mature in the faith, our picture and understanding of Jesus becomes fuller and more inclusive.

We discover that the more we think we know about Jesus, the more we realize we have to learn. As soon as we think we have Jesus in our hearts as a gentle shepherd, we experience an angry man upturning tables in the temple and attacking the religious economic system. As soon as we think we have Jesus accepting everyone who comes to him, we see him refusing (at first) to cast out the demons of the daughter of the Syro-Phoenician woman. As soon as we think that Jesus is not confrontational, we hear him saying, "Woe to you …" All of these pictures we have of Jesus, of God, are in the Gospel accounts. They are all true.

Let's look at just a few of the truths we know about Jesus, our Savior and our Lord. We know that Jesus came to do the will of the Father who sent him. The Father's will, as proclaimed by the prophets, called for justice for all who were poor, powerless, marginalized, and oppressed. We know that Jesus reached out to lepers, widows, and the lame. He said to give food to the hungry, drink to the thirsty, and clothing to people who have none. Jesus instructed us to care for sick people and visit the imprisoned, so we can know them. The God of Israel, as well as God revealed in Jesus, willed life, health, and compassion for all, especially those the rest of us would like to ignore. How many people in our communities have no medical insurance, or inadequate insurance, or cannot access the services available? In other words, how many people in our communities are medically underserved? Are we walking the way of Jesus?

Jesus came to announce and inaugurate the kingdom of God. I know a woman who says, "When I am queen of the world …" and then says some outrageous thing like "Cars will have roads just for them high above the highways where trucks must drive." Well, Jesus came and declared to us that God is ruler of the world and then proceeded to describe that kingdom to us.

Jesus said the kingdom of God:

> is like a mustard seed, which, when sown upon the
> ground, is the smallest of all the seeds on earth; yet
> when it is sown it grows up and becomes the greatest
> of all shrubs, … so that the birds of the air can make
> nests in its shade." (Mark 4:31–32)

Jesus said about the kingdom of God:

> "It is easier for a camel to go through the eye of a
> needle than for someone who is rich to enter the
> kingdom of God." [The disciples] were greatly
> astounded and said to one another, "Then who
> can be saved?" Jesus looked at them and said, "For
> mortals it is impossible, but not for God; for God all
> things are possible." (Mark 10:25–27)

On another occasion, Jesus described the kingdom of God this way:

> Do not keep striving for what you are to eat and
> what you are to drink, and do not keep worrying. …
> Instead, strive for [your Father's] kingdom, and these
> things will be given to you as well. (Luke 12:29, 31)

Are we living as kingdom of God people when a minimum wage worker, earning $5.85 an hour, can afford monthly rent of no more than $304 a month? What is the fair market rent for a two-bedroom apartment in your community? $500? $700? $1,000? More?

Are we walking the way of Jesus?

Jesus was the friend of sinful people who did not adhere to the prevailing religious standards or those who were outcasts because of illness, gender, or occupation. Think of the parable of the Good Samaritan when the church folks passed by a wounded victim of highway robbery who was lying on the road. A Samaritan, who was considered to be a half-breed, a subhuman, took care of the victim. Jesus became ritually unclean when he touched lepers, bleeding women, or dead people. He was a friend to the ones society at best ignores and at worst, tortures. How many people in our communities live in poverty? In multicultural environments, are there economic disparities among the different racial and ethnic groups? Are we too busy going about our daily routines to notice and reach out to those who are invisible in our communities?

Are we walking the way of Jesus?

Jesus believed that caring for people who were hurting was more important than adhering to religious standards or dogmas. Jesus healed on the Sabbath—*horrors!* He taught, "You have heard that it was said, 'An eye for an eye and a tooth for a tooth.' But I say to you, 'Do not resist an evildoer. But if anyone strikes you on the right cheek, turn the other also'" (Matthew 5:38–39). Paul says it another way: "If I have prophetic powers, and understand all mysteries and all knowledge, and if I have all faith, so as to remove mountains, but do not have love, I am nothing" (1 Corinthians 13:2).

Are we walking the way of Jesus?

Jesus came to give his life as "a ransom for many" (Matthew 20:28) to help people know how to live in deep relationship with God and with one another. Jesus arguably worked for reconciliation with his enemies. If Jesus is this way, why in the world cannot we as followers of Jesus also work for reconciliation wherever it is needed—in our home, our congregation, our community, our state, our country, and our world?

Are we walking the way of Jesus? Jesus said, "I am the way, the truth, and the life." Do we really live this, or do we only say the words? Lenore Chambers [7] challenges us with her poem:

> An old time prophet might record,
> Thus saith the Lord:
> 'Pharisee, Sadducee, Priest, and Scribe.
> Where were you when my son died?
> Crossing t's and dotting i's,
> Is it right to circumcise?
> Angels and demons, oral tradition,
> Purity, sanctity, and verbal rendition.
> Debating authority, self-willing humanity.

Dissecting me with theology.
Accuse, defend, argue, scheme —
The important things remain unseen.
With barbed words and poisoned tongues
Attitudes aren't changed.
All the talk to justify
Still leaves you all estranged.
Analyze, categorize, stigmatize.
Don't you realize?
The Body's broken
By the chosen.
Noisy gongs and clanging cymbals!
How blind can you be?
All of your correctness is dismembering me.
I left you instructions, I gave you my will.
I gave you each other to love and fulfill.
I am the way, the truth, and the life.
I'll not be your excuse for constant strife.
Stop all your bickering, there's work to be done.
When it's time for a judge, I'll be the one.
Oh Pharisee, Sadducee, Priest and Scribe
Where were you when Jesus died?

And the remarkable thing is ... Jesus loves us anyway. Jesus loves me, this I know. For the Bible tells me so. I too can love, and so can you.

Questions to Consider

1. How does this treatment of Jesus as the way, the truth, and the life challenge you?

2. How would your Christian community answer, "Are we walking the way of Jesus?"

3. Is there a call from God for you in this passage? If so, what is it?

4. How does walking the way of Jesus affect how you love your neighbor?

5. Having looked at this passage now, you will never be the same again. Do you agree or disagree? So what now?

Prayer

God of right relationships, you know that some in our community are so ill from addictions, mental illness, or fatigue in trying to survive that they have given up. Others are homeless and believe that no one cares and that their lives can't be any different.

Forgive us for our apathy for their hurting and their pain. We often choose literally to look the other way. We make policies that indicate that we consider them as nuisances rather than as your chosen sons and daughters. We believe ourselves to be better than they. In our arrogance, we forget that some of us were born to families that could help us become successful as the world measures success. We ignore that for some of us the color of our skin brings us benefits that we simply take for granted. We assume that everyone sees the world as we see it with the advantages of financial resources, education, community contacts, and power.

God of all people, instill in us the compassion that Jesus the Christ embodied. Break our hearts so that we will be your heart in our community. Give us burning eyes so that we can finally see all our neighbors through your eyes. Make our feet itch so we will walk with you where homeless people walk. Drag us into being good disciples who put flesh on caring words and actions onto pious proclamations.

We profess to be your children and your followers. Convict us to live into our statements of faith. You are our God. We glorify you, we praise you, and we honor you.

In love we pray. Amen

Chapter Four

Requirements of Faith

Micah 2:1–11; 6:6–8

*What does the LORD require of you but to do justice, and to love
kindness, and to walk humbly with your God? (Micah 6:8)*

W HEN I BEGAN WORKING with this passage, I was not expecting
to be poked between the eyes with the timeliness and the
utter directness of Micah. This scripture moves us beyond seeing
poverty as the fault of the person who is poor to realizing that the way
our society organizes itself, in fact, causes some of that poverty.

Whenever I'm working with prophets' proclamations in one of
the shorter books in the Old Testament called minor prophets, I look
at the book as a whole. It is usually not a big deal since most of them
are only three or four chapters long. A few, like Zechariah, which has
fourteen chapters, are longer.

So I started reading Micah. I got to Micah 2:2. The prophet wrote,
"They covet fields, and seize them; houses, and take them away; they
oppress the householder and house, people and their inheritance."
This verse hints of our process of eminent domain or maybe even
gentrification when those of us with resources buy up land and houses
cheap, convert them to beautiful properties, revel in our good fortune
and smart business sense, and get rid of the people who have struggled
in the area forever. Even if we do not intend to push out the people who
have lived in the neighborhood a long time, the increase in property

taxes resulting from the increased viability of the neighborhood means they can no longer afford to live in their family home.

A neighborhood near a major hospital has long been neglected. The houses are tiny and often in poor repair. In fact, many have been condemned and destroyed. Other houses are boarded up and abandoned to the homeless people who sneak in to sleep and conduct unsavory business. Longtime residents have been holding on through the years of the city's looking the other way. One lady walks daily to the hospital where she works as a housekeeper. For years she has been able to meet the basic needs of herself and her family because she's been able to get to her job. However, the neighborhood is being rebuilt. The homes which are rising from the ground are lovely. Some will be purchased by young professionals who will live in them. Others will be offered for rent. Unfortunately she will not be able to benefit from the new homes. She is barely holding her life together in her current home. She asks, "What's going to happen to me? I cannot afford these new places. If I have to move, how will I get to work?" She has been self-sufficient until now but wonders if she will be able to continue when others move into her neighborhood.

It sounds as if Micah has heard her lament.

I have an idea that some of you might agree with Micah 2:6b when the people say, "One should not preach of such things; disgrace will not overtake us." You wish I would not write about neighborhoods that are being improved so much that the people who live there are no longer welcome. You may plead, "Please don't highlight what Micah points out as affronts to God by quoting Micah 2:1–11; 3; 6:7; or 6:9–16." I don't blame you. I don't like hearing it either ... but it is *in* the Bible. It is part of our holy scriptures.

You might like Micah's words in 2:11: "If someone were to go about uttering empty falsehoods, saying, 'I will preach to you of wine and strong drink,' such a one would be the preacher for this people!" Yeah, now we're talking! Forget poverty. Let's talk about real sin, like public drunkenness.

Micah 2:8–9 states: "But you rise up against my people as an enemy; you strip the robe from the peaceful, from those who pass by trustingly with no thought of war. The women of my people you drive out from their pleasant houses; from their young children you take away my glory forever." As we regularly hear the drums of war from our news media and redevelop neighborhoods leaving people homeless, we become acutely aware of the timeliness of Micah's charge.

Chapter 3 doesn't get much better. Micah in 3:9–11 exhorts: "Hear this, you rulers of the house of Jacob and chiefs of the house of Israel, who abhor justice and pervert all equity, who build Zion with blood and Jerusalem with wrong! Its rulers give judgment for a bribe, its priests teach for a price, its prophets give oracles for money; yet they lean upon the LORD and say, 'Surely the LORD is with us! No harm shall come upon us.'" If I expand on this one, I'm really going to get into trouble, so I'll let you draw your own parallels with the contemporary scene.

I need to stop quoting the prophet Micah. It is no surprise that prophets were often killed, laughed at, or thrown into prison.

Micah's description of powerful people stomping on powerless people is the context for those paraphrased words of 6:6–8: "Do justice, love kindness, and walk humbly with your God." which are often printed in beautiful script, framed elegantly, and hung in places where they can be seen for inspiration.

"Do justice, love kindness, and walk humbly with your God."

Let's look first at "justice." We often use "justice" as a legal term. But "justice" in the Bible can have another meaning. To understand the biblical use of the term "justice," we must talk about *shalom*, because justice and *shalom* are closely related in scripture. *Shalom* is often translated as "peace." When we say peace, we usually mean an absence of conflict or a placid state of being.

The holy scriptures have a different understanding of *shalom*. The term *shalom* in the Bible points us to balance in the community … balance between haves and have-nots, between those with power and those without, between young and old, and between citizens and sojourners. *Shalom* is about healed, healthy, balanced, and happy relationships between individuals, between people and God, and between people and nature.

Justice then means turning *shalom* into reality. Marcus Borg says that "most often in the Bible, the opposite of God's justice is not God's mercy but human injustice."[8] The Golden Rule, "Do unto others as you would have them do unto you," is a brief statement of creating *shalom* or a rule of justice. It provides a test: "Would I want this to happen to me and mine? If I don't, then why in the world will I tolerate it happening to others or to those people?"

We are to do justice.

Then we are to "love kindness." I prefer *mercy*, another word which is often used here in translations. We are to love mercy. I did a spot survey with people I know and asked them to define "mercy." Everyone I asked was reared in the church and still considered themselves to be devout. However, each of them struggled to give me a definition. One said, "Forgiveness." He said, "When I think of mercy, I often think of letting people off the hook. They are forgiven, and they do not have to pay any consequences for their actions." Another person said that mercy was what we owed a criminal because no one committed a crime who was not in some way a victim too. Someone else said, "Mercy means 'Don't punish me even though I deserve to be punished.'"

What is the understanding of mercy for the faithful person who wants to be in close relationship with God? Jesus himself quoted Hosea 6:6 when he said, "Those who are well have no need of a physician, but those who are sick. Go and learn what this means. 'I desire mercy, not sacrifice'" (Matthew 9:12–13). What makes this quote fascinating is that the same quote in Hosea is translated in the New Revised Standard Version of the Bible as: "I desire steadfast love and not sacrifice." Steadfast love … mercy … steadfast love. This is where we get close to the meaning of mercy. Steadfast love, love as God loves. When we are merciful, we imitate God. We love as God loves.

To love this way is not an emotion, a wave of pity, or even looking the other way when someone does something wrong. Being merciful means that we actively and deliberately try to reflect God's love and grace to another. Having this kind of love means we define ourselves in terms of community rather than in terms of our individual needs and wants. Mercy is a term of relationship. To love mercy means to try to see the situation, the reality, through the eyes of the other person. Mercy means understanding that the high-school dropout left school because her mother was dead, her father was chronically and desperately ill, and there was no one else to care for him. Mercy means realizing that the prostitute on the street was sexually abused as a child, and her boyfriend pushed her into prostitution to support his habit. She was so starved for his attention or was so afraid of him that she did what he demanded and got caught up in a life beyond her control. To love mercy entails entering the other person's perceptions so that we can experience the situation as he or she does. This kind of identification is not a feeling. It is an intentional choice of alignment with another.

Another way to consider mercy is to look at its opposites—in other words, what mercy is *not*. Mercy is not an "-ism." It is not racism, classism, or sexism. We love regardless of skin color, ethnicity, social or economic standing, gender, or sexual orientation. Mercy comes from our understanding that God faithfully maintains covenant responsibility with the people whom God loves. As God loves us, so we are to love one another. We are to be merciful as God is merciful. We are to love, comfort, and aid one another. We experience God's love as a gracious gift, and we are to reflect that grace to other people.

Does this mean that we are to look the other way when someone does something wrong or when someone angers us? No, it means that when we chastise or when we say no, we do it with steadfast love and grace. We hold others accountable for their actions, all the while pulling for and planning with them for their growth and health with steadfast love. We get in the other person's skin. We try to see from their perspective.

In God's mercy, God became human to demonstrate in action for us what mercy means. It means loving and caring for and confronting those who take advantage of other people. Mercy means listening to God rather than the powers of the world. God's kind of mercy means protecting the abandoned, leading the enslaved to freedom, calling forth new ways of relating to God and God's creation, and leading people to centeredness and a sense of belonging. God is with us still, calling us to be merciful.

Being merciful is not easy for us. God calls us to relate with other people and with God. God calls us to live and love in a world of *shalom*—peace, balance, and harmony. Yet our world is one of authority and domination. In our world individualism abounds over community. We do not easily relate to one another. We relate only to those whom we like, those with whom we are comfortable, or those with whom we have a lot in common. We all suffer to some extent from xenophobia, the fear of the stranger. In our world we want to look good, to live well, and to be safe.

When we do justice and love mercy then, inevitably, we "walk humbly" with our God. We walk with God. Isn't that the bottom line for those of us who profess faith in Jesus Christ…to walk with God?

We know what we need to do. We even know how to do it. What seems to be missing is our will to do justice, love mercy, and walk humbly with our God. For this, we pray to God to be with us in our attempts to live as God's people. For this, we meet together to encourage each other on our journey. For this, we ask forgiveness when we fail. For this, we praise God for loving us anyway and for offering us more opportunities to show how much we love—by doing justice, loving mercy, and walking humbly with our God.

Questions to Consider

1. Is the bottom line for you to walk with God? If so, what does that mean for you?

2. Does thinking about mercy as loving-kindness open up any new ideas for you?

3. How do we engage our will to do justice, love mercy, and walk humbly with God?

4. Do the Micah verses issue a call to action for you personally? If so, what is the call?

5. Read Micah 6:6–8. Now that you have reflected on this passage, you will never be the same again. Do you agree or disagree? Why?

6. Does this passage affect how you love your neighbor? If it does, how?

Prayer

Loving God, Holy One of our lives, we come to you with our heads bowed in shame. We have brothers and sisters who have no place to call home who walk these very streets. We choose not to see them, or we decide that they want to live in Dumpsters or in bamboo thickets. We wash our hands of them, and we sweep our streets of them. We are afraid of people who remind us that life is as unstable as cardboard-box houses. We study the causes, make our pronouncements, write our laws, design our policies ... and we forget.

Creator of the universe, we forget the people whom you might call the "least of these." You remember the birds of the air and the lilies of the field—but we forget our sisters and brothers. Thrust your call to care on us, so we cannot forget.

Open our eyes that we can see the world as you see it. Shake us up that we can feel the hurts that surround us. Alert us to the ways we thwart your good intent for all people in our communities. Remove the scales from our hearts that we can remove the burdens we place on people. Strengthen our legs that we can lift people up and not squash them down. Wrap us in courage that we can reach out to the strange among us and love them as you love them.

God of the downtrodden, we ask now the most challenging thing of all. Turn us around that we may learn from homeless and poor people and celebrate what they can teach us about themselves as well as about ourselves and who you are. Once we see through their eyes, sear your truth in our hearts that we may amass all the power and resources at our disposal to serve those whom you most care for: those who have no power or resources. Make us aware of the unexpected ways you continue to come to us. You have revealed yourself in the past in a burning bush, a pillar of cloud, a baby in a manger, and an itinerant rabbi. Why not a ragged, smelly man who looks in our eyes?

Help us to see you, care for you, and love you, our God, who was yourself homeless. Lead us to be your partner in claiming our community as your Holy Place.

In Christ's name we pray, Amen.

Chapter Five
Poverty in the Bible

W<small>E OFTEN THINK ABOUT</small> poverty as living with inadequate financial resources. Indeed, when asked to tell one story from the Bible which depicts a poor person, many people immediately tell Jesus' parable of the Good Samaritan (Luke 10:30–37). This Samaritan, who was considered by many at the time to be a nobody (or worse), stops to help a victim of roadside violence. What makes his service remarkable is that religious authorities walking past the poor man have ignored his plight. The good neighbor, the Samaritan, even pays for ongoing care for the person he's assisted. This is certainly a wonderful example for how we are to reach out to others.

However, there are other stories in the Bible that also involve people who lack resources—money, power, health, position, etc. If you decide to do this study in a group and the group is large, you might divide into smaller groups to consider the following passages. Groups may choose to study as many as they feel can be addressed in the time allotted. You will find questions to consider at the end of the list. [9]

Hagar, the Egyptian	Genesis 16:1–6, 21:1–21
Sarah	Genesis 20: 1–7
Jacob and his family	Genesis 42:1–46:7
Moses' family	Exodus 1:8–2:10
The Levite's concubine	Judges 19:1–30

Ruth	Ruth
Uriah	2 Samuel 11:2–12:23
Naboth	1 Kings 21:1–16
The widow	2 Kings 4:1–7
The sons of the prophets	1 Kings 4:38–44
Esther	Esther
Job	Job
The Canaanite woman	Matthew 15:21–28
The children	Matthew 19:13–15
The two blind men	Matthew 20:29–34
Sheep and goats	Matthew 25:31–46
The demoniac	Mark 5:1–20
The widow and her mite	Mark 12:41–44
The widow of Nain	Luke 7:11–17
The woman with flow of blood	Luke 8:43–48
The good Samaritan	Luke 10:25–37
The woman and her lost coin	Luke 15:8–10
The prodigal son	Luke 15:11–32
Lazarus	Luke 16:19–31
The man born blind	John 9:1–41

Questions to consider

1. Why or how are the people poor?

2. Poverty is more than financial. What other kinds of poverty are spoken of in the Bible: Powerlessness? Health? Hunger? Victimization? Other?

3. Which of these biblical characters chose to be poor?

4. How did their society respond to the people in these stories? Do any of the responses align with your understanding of sacred covenant with God?

For the Journey
Poverty and the Faithful Person

Litany from Proverbs

Leader: Do not rob the poor because they are poor, or crush the afflicted at the gate;

People: *For the* LORD *pleads their cause and despoils of life those who despoil them* (22:22–23).

Leader: Do not remove an ancient landmark or encroach on the fields of orphans;

People: *For their redeemer is strong; he will plead their cause against you* (23:10–11).

Leader: If you hold back from rescuing those taken away to death, those who go staggering to the slaughter;

People: *... Does not he who keeps watch over your soul know it? And will he not repay all according their deeds* (24:11–12)?

Leader: If you close your ear to the cry of the poor,

People: *You will cry out and not be heard* (21:13).

Leader: Those who are generous are blessed,

People: *For they share their bread with the poor* (22:9).

Leader: The righteous know the rights of the poor;

People: *The wicked have no such understanding* (29:7).

Leader: Those who despise their neighbor are sinners,

People: *But happy are those who are kind to the poor* (14:21).

Leader: Those who oppress the poor insult their Maker,

People: *But those who are kind to the needy honor him* (14:31).

Leader: Whoever is kind to the poor lends to the LORD,

People: *And will be repaid in full* (19:17).

Leader: She opens her hand to the poor,

People: *And reaches out her hands to the needy* (31:20).

Leader: If a king judges the poor with equity,

People: *His throne will be established forever* (29:14).

Leader: Speak out, judge righteously,

People: *Defend the rights of the poor and needy* (31:9).

Leader: The LORD tears down the house of the proud,

People: *But maintains the widow's boundaries* (15:25).

Leader: Like a roaring lion or a charging bear
People: *Is a wicked ruler over a poor people* (28:15).
Leader: Speak out for those who cannot speak ....
People: *Defend the rights of the poor and needy* (31:8–9).
Leader: To do righteousness and justice
People: *Is more acceptable to the LORD than sacrifice* (21:3).

Part Two:

A Thoughtful Approach to Deciding How, When, and Whom to Help

Chapter Six

When Someone in Need Approaches You

*A*FTER WE HAVE STUDIED scripture passages and strengthened our resolve to reach out to others, we may come to a stop about what to do next. Our heart may be warm with compassion, our will may be intent on helping people in poverty, and our hands may itch to do something positive for someone. But our thoughts may say: "Okay. But how do I do this? How do I reach out in ways that truly help? How can I be sure what I do does not give someone drug money? What do I say? I don't know, so maybe I just won't do anything." Now we move into practical tips and thoughtful approaches for helping our neighbors who live with poverty. Now we take our holy call and put feet to it.

First of all, let's consider why people beg. *Why?* Because it works. [10] When we are confronted with helping someone who walks up to us on the street and asks for money, we have a variety of responses. Some truly may be a blessing to the person who is seeking a handout, and others may be destructive. Unfortunately we often believe we have only two possibilities: give the money or suggest by word or action that we do not care.

Giving Money Directly

When someone walks up to us, tells us his or her "situation," and asks for money, we may pull out cash and give it. We do it because we truly want to help. Or else we give because we feel guilty. We respond because we are afraid. We hand over money because we want the person to go away. We tell ourselves we do not judge the true depth of their need. Sometimes we help because we, too, have been in a similar situation, or one of our family members is currently living on the street. Sometimes we let others know of our generosity—although we may sound a little sheepish as we wonder if we did the right thing. We acknowledge that we may have been taken advantage of.

As long as we keep pulling money out of our pockets for any of the above reasons, people will continue to solicit or beg on the streets. It works! When we hand over money on the street to someone who asks, we allow begging to flourish in our community. We are to blame.

What about those folks who hold up signs that say, "Will work for food"? Are the needs real? Maybe. But think about where we see these folks. They are usually on corners in prosperous socioeconomic areas, near major shopping areas or at intersections near high-end neighborhoods. They are in locations where drivers are likely to hand over money with no questions asked. We may see the same person day after day. Wouldn't *someone* have offered him or her a job? It is so easy to pull alongside, roll down the window of our car, and hand out five dollars. We tell ourselves that we care and that we are being a good model for our children. However, next time notice the shoes of the people who have the signs. Do the shoes confirm a financial need or a readiness to work?

Some people might categorize a person who voiced these kinds of concerns as an uncaring so-and-so. This is not true. People of faith who have worked a long time with people in need and who passionately believe in caring for hurting, struggling, and abandoned people want to create environments that assist those who desire to improve their situations. Handouts on the street are probably not the best way to do that.

A Better Way to Respond

The second half of the Bible verse in Matthew 10:16 is helpful: "Be wise as serpents and innocent as doves."

In being "wise as serpents," we acknowledge that giving cash may not help but instead may actually hurt. This money might reward begging rather than honest work. It might be used to purchase illegal substances or services. On the other hand, it might indeed buy needed medications or food.

Being wise means giving the money—but to organizations that can truly help someone. There are agencies and social service ministries in your community able to offer life-changing opportunities to folks. They can provide solutions to the problems and issues that resulted in people needing to ask for handouts. When you support helpful organizations, you can suggest one of them to someone who asks you for money. Such organizations include:

- Soup kitchens providing at least one meal every day of the week.
- Night shelters providing places to sleep—not as comfortable as a motel room, but shelter until the person can do better.
- Cooperative ministries or community action groups helping people with rent, utilities, or food.
- Agencies helping people get a job or provide a process to earn their GED.
- Case management services connecting program participants to mental health services, addiction treatment programs, and other assistance needed to move into long-term housing.

With organizations in many of our communities ready and able to help people who are motivated to improve their situations, we short-circuit true opportunity for those who come up to us on the street. As long as we continue to give money directly, we prevent the asker from seeking long-term solutions. We indeed help the person continue as a beggar rather than encourage him or her to do what is necessary to take charge of life in a healthy way.

Giving Money for Long-Term Solutions, Not "Quick Fixes"

Consider making a significant contribution to the agency of your choice, at least as much as you would normally give from your wallet when approached for a handout. When someone comes to you and asks for money, rather than reaching into your pocket and pulling out change or a dollar bill, look the person in the eye, thereby acknowledging his or her value as a human being. Then say, "I care about you. I'm not going to give you money. I support 'Agency's Name.' I know they can help you beyond anything I have to offer. Go see them."

You'll have to practice a bit to be comfortable with this way of saying "no" to the immediate request *and* "yes" to longer-lasting solutions. This way of helping improves the quality of life for all of us.

Summing Up

When you financially support an organization in your community that works with people who are homeless, destitute, or needy, you provide significant assistance for the program participants who use their services. Helping agencies, human service organizations, and faith-based ministries address people's immediate needs. Some of them go even deeper and enable program participants to confront the deep challenges that led to their homelessness or severe poverty. They use the funds you give—funds you otherwise might have given on the street—to provide long-term assistance. When someone asks you directly for money, you can establish contact by looking him or her in the eye, conveying that you care, and because you care, you support an agency that can help for the long term. You help so people do not have to be out on the street begging for money. They have long-term solutions available to them—if they just use them.

Questions to Consider

1. Why do you give money to someone who comes up to you on the street? Are you motivated by compassion? Do you want the person simply to go away?

2. Think of a time when you gave money to a "beggar." Would you do it again? Why or why not?

3. How do local agencies in your community handle what's often called "panhandling"? How does your local government approach this issue? Do you agree with the procedures?

Chapter Seven
Helping Others: Servant or Sucker?

*T*HROUGH THE YEARS, I have learned that people truly do want to help others. They share stories with me of how they have reached out with all good intentions. However, they have felt as if they were taken advantage of ... "suckered!" They may have been clueless about what to do. They may have gotten angry at the very people they wanted to help.

We really can serve other people without feeling as if we've been suckered ... most of the time. When we better understand the people we want to help, when we are clear in our intentions for helping, and when we clarify for ourselves what we will and will not do, then we can offer significant and powerful assistance to the people we choose to care for.

The Reality of Being Suckered

Most of us have probably had the feeling that we have been suckered when we were truly trying to help someone. We may have given money to someone begging on the street and wondered whether we were helping with a serious need *or* if we were giving money for the next drug buy. We may have given a bag of food and then seen the recipient selling the items in the bag to the guy down the street. We may have spoken to the woman who hangs out in the doorway of our church and even brought her coffee and a Danish on occasion. After months of connecting with her in a real

53

way, she may have stolen from us. We may have helped someone with a need one time and then discovered that we were now expected to continue to give and give and give … with few questions asked.

Many ministers and leaders in congregations have had the experience of preparing to walk into the biggest wedding of the year, and at this most inopportune time, someone comes up and says he needs money for getting to his grandmother's funeral, buying medication, whatever. What happens? The church leader reaches into his pocket and pulls out whatever cash is there, hands over the money, and quickly sends the person on his way.

When we give this way, is our motivation to help in the manner of Jesus? Are we offering help with true compassion to a sister or brother in Christ? Probably not. Our intent for giving the money is simply to get rid of the person. "Just go away." We don't do true ministry. We send a negative message.

The scripture passages highlighted in Part One reminded us that we are called to reach out to others with compassion. We are to be involved in helping them become the people God created and is still creating them to be. If we feel we have been "suckered" when trying to help others, we might decide that we will not help again and may even become proponents of tough measures that prevent people from being able to change their lives. People who feel they've been taken advantage of by someone with issues of addiction may argue that "those people" need to be locked up for using drugs inappropriately rather than helped in overcoming the power of the drug. When we have been disenchanted by trying to reach out and help, we might exclaim, "Those people are all losers. No matter what we do, they'll never change. They will always be the same!"

As natural as these reactions might be, we as people of faith believe in the hope of new life. Our Lord Jesus died and was resurrected, thus proving that death and destruction are not the last word for any person or any situation. People of faith believe in redemption. We believe that the old can be made new. People of faith proclaim a Savior who reached out to those despised and ignored by society.

We truly want to help. We just don't want to feel we've been suckered.

Trying to Understand Those We Want to Help

When we try to understand the situations of people who are poor, we can reach out to them in more loving ways. When we are willing to set aside our own realities so that we can see the world through the eyes of the people we want to help, we are wiser and more loving and compassionate.

Moving beyond our own ways of thinking and acting is challenging. We ask, "My way works for me; why won't it work for them?" Let's look at that. When we intend to work with people who are poor, we need to put aside our value system, our moral system, and how we make decisions in order to be truly present to the people who come seeking our help. People who are from different socioeconomic situations, who are educated differently, or who are from a different race or culture do not approach life, solutions, and situations in the same way we do. We understand this when we travel to other countries or even other ethnic neighborhoods in our area. We sense that our ways of thinking about things may make little sense to those whose environs we are visiting. People who are different by race, socioeconomics, or education challenge us to take ourselves out of the center as the reference point for what should happen, how it should happen, and when it should happen—and that is extremely difficult to do.

The easiest way to think about stepping out of our center is to assume a person from China is visiting. (Note: This works only if you are not Chinese!) We would not expect her to have the same value system, have the same moral system, or make decisions the same way we do because she is from a different culture. The same is true of the people we might want to assist. The cultural difference may be socioeconomic, racial/ethnic, or related to education. One of us might be from a relatively healthy family, and one of us from an unhealthy family. Whatever the specifics, we are reaching across a cultural divide.

Just as a Chinese person might use English words differently from the way we use them, people without resources use certain words differently from the way people with resources use those same words. For example, consider the word *time*. Those of us with resources can think in long blocks of time. We can think about vacations set to happen in a few months. We can think about retirement. However, people without resources think about time differently. For example, we might ask someone, "How long did you keep your last job?" The person may reply, "I kept it a long time!" "How long was that?" "Oh, two months!"

Two months for people with resources is not a long time at all. But when you have resources, you have no concerns about a roof over your head, food on your table, health care for your children, and other amenities often taken for granted in our culture. If you have experienced loss of electricity during an ice storm, for example, you can begin to relate. The four nights and five days without power seemed a much longer time than four nights and five days with power.

Another word is *money*. Those with resources understand the word *money* to mean security. It means home, food, health care, and a retirement plan. To those without resources, the word *money* means more than food on the table or resources to pay the rent. It means "having the good life." This is why a teacher might do a home visit and find a gigantic television in the room. It was likely installed with a ten-dollars-down/ten-dollars-a-week plan. The television provides entertainment. It explains why a child might be on free or reduced lunch at school and still have an MP3 player. Money means having the good life.

Dr. Ruby Payne in *A Framework for Understanding Poverty* [11] breaks the population into three distinct socioeconomic groups. The first she calls Generational Poverty which includes households who have lived in poverty for at least two generations. These are not necessarily welfare families. In the area of the country where I live, these families might have lived in back coves in the mountains or in mill villages for several generations. Payne speaks also of the Middle Class and Wealth socioeconomic groups. Each group has different values:

> Poverty values: entertainment and relationships
> Middle Class values: work and achievement
> Wealth values: social networks that can help make
> things happen

One can see that approaching solutions from a work and achievement orientation would call forth different solutions than a focus on entertainment and relationships. Each set of values is important for the folks in a particular level of resources but may not easily translate to another socioeconomic group. What works for survival and success in one group might not work in another.

Note: The exercise at the end of this chapter will expand your understanding of the challenges of educational and socioeconomic differences.

Techniques You Can Adopt: Mantras, The Three Vs, the A-B-Cs, and L.E.A.R.N.

Let's talk about tools which will help you develop your skills in discerning how to help. Certain mantras can help you stay connected without getting engulfed in another's problems. Remembering the three Vs will guide your direct assistance without inadvertently helping someone in negative ways. The A-B-Cs of helping will clarify your conversations with people who are seeking help. L.E.A.R.N. will help you learn to say no in loving and compassionate ways that provide significant help even though you do not address the specific stated need.

Mantras

Once you have committed to helping others with thought, care, compassion, and wisdom, these mantras can prove helpful as you reach out to your neighbor in loving ways.

1. Do not ever do something for people that they can and should do for themselves.

When we perceive that someone needs our help, it is extremely tempting to do a lot for the person. We act from our compassion. But we may inadvertently give the message that we do not believe the recipient of our attention can handle life. For example, when we make a phone call for someone who is capable of dialing the number, we have indicated that we are more capable than she is. If necessary, we can sit with her and coach her if we are not certain she can handle the details of a conversation. By helping her complete a difficult task, we instill pride in her. When we suggest she cannot be in charge of her life, guess what? She will often begin to prove us right!

There may be times when we realize we are working harder on a person's life issues than he is—which is not healthy or healing for either of us. What we are about is helping him claim the fullness of his humanity as a child of God. We want to help him become the person God intends him to be.

2. Poor planning on your part does not constitute an emergency on my part.

People in need know only their need. For them, getting us to do whatever they need or want us to do right now becomes very important. If they need food, they want it now. If their power is going to be turned off today, they need us to pay that bill *today*. However, that does not *necessarily* mean we need to work on their time schedule.

For example, a woman may show up at a church and say, "I have a cutoff notice for today. If you don't pay my bill, my power will be cut off at five o'clock!" Let's consider that scenario. People usually have time before they receive a disconnect notice to seek appropriate assistance in paying their bill. Where I live, a power bill is for electricity used during the previous thirty days. If I do not pay the bill that month, the next bill I receive includes two months of power already used (past due month and the previous month). The only portion which I must pay to prevent disconnection of service is the past due month's bill. If I do not pay that, then I will receive a disconnect notice. By then I may have used almost three months of power without paying. Waiting until the very last minute is not a necessity in that scenario. *Poor planning on your part does not constitute an emergency on mine.*

United Ministries' Place of Hope, a day center in Greenville, South Carolina, offers showers, a mailing address, a telephone, and washers and dryers to people who are homeless. Program participants also receive help in addressing the issues that led to their homelessness.

When the center first opened, a homeless person might come in and ask the staff to help him move into a place to live. The caseworker would search for a cheap place to rent and then help the person move in by paying deposits, by purchasing furniture from a thrift store, or by seeking donations. After all, the intention of the day center staff was to move homeless people off the streets. Unfortunately by responding to the immediate request, the "emergency," the caseworker had not laid a solid foundation for success with the homeless person. In just a few weeks, the person was once again homeless. The donated furniture collected to furnish the new apartment was dumped on the side of the street, the deposits for rent and utilities were lost, and a landlord had lost faith in the staff of the Place of Hope. There was no plan with the homeless program participant for ongoing stability.

Today, before addressing the issue of housing, the caseworker assesses the problems that underlie the person's homelessness. The Place of Hope staff members build a relationship with program participants and assess their commitment to confront their issues. The staff may ask for some signs of readiness: keeping appointments, bringing back literature from another program, or carrying out a simple assignment. The caseworker and the participant converse intensely and regularly to develop a long-term plan involving life-changing opportunities before either of them places phone calls to other agencies which can help.

Is the underlying problem addiction? Is it mental illness? Is it disability? Are there legal issues? Those questions are addressed first. The staff person or volunteer assists the program participant into appropriate programs offered by mental health centers, addiction treatment facilities, legal services, and other organizations which can help. Then—and only then—does the staff member help move the program participant into long-term housing. Instead of helping only one or two people a year attain stability, today one out of six people who enter the Place of Hope moves into long-term housing. Well-thought-out planning—instead of measures to meet an immediate "emergency"—is the key to opening up long-term, real solutions to the chronic problems of the most needy people among us.

3. Be wise as serpents and innocent as doves.

This is the second half of the Bible verse found in Matthew 10:16. In this passage, Jesus is instructing his disciples before sending them out on the road. It is a particularly fitting admonition for those of us who feel called by our loving God to reach out to people in need: people who are often ignored by society but whom God loves passionately.

In being "wise as serpents," we learn all we can about the realities and conditions of the people we are striving to serve. We are real in our interactions with them. So, for example, if someone tells us that she has had a number of jobs in the past year, we might delve into the reasons she has not kept a position. If she replies, "For absenteeism," our next response might be, "Oh, tell me about your addiction issues." At that point, she may inform us that her absenteeism was related to something else, but we have opened the door to ongoing, substantive dialogue. In being wise as serpents, we might challenge in a gentle yet firm way when someone tells us a tale which simply does not make sense. I've been known to respond upon hearing something which was unbelievable, "Do you think I was born yesterday?"

Those of us who were raised with good manners, and especially those of us raised in the South, might find this kind of retort to be offensive and rude. What I have discovered (and had confirmed repeatedly) is that calling something as we see it and naming some action as truthfully as we can garners us amazing credibility. The other person believes we know what we are doing, that we are indeed trustworthy, and that we can truly help.

The second part of the verse, "and innocent as doves," means that whatever we say must be spoken with care and compassion. We can be firm *and* kind. We can learn to say no and still receive a sincere hug and word of thanks because we treated someone with empathy and as a person with value.

Of course, you will not say the mantras out loud to someone who is seeking your assistance. You can, however, keep these in the back of your mind as you assess the request and the situation:

> *1. Do not ever do something for people that they can and should do for themselves.*
> *2. Poor planning on your part does not constitute an emergency on my part.*
> *3. Be wise as serpents and innocent as doves.*

You can ask yourself, "Can this person handle this alone?" "Is this a real emergency or a symptom of poor planning?" "Am I being wise?"

"Am I being loving?" The mantras will help you be mindful of your intention to love your neighbor in truly caring ways.

The Three Vs

Another tool in discerning how to help is the Three Vs. This tool will enable you to provide assistance with financial resources without inadvertently helping someone in negative ways. By following the Three Vs, you will be less likely to give resources that may be converted into drugs or other death-dealing commodities.

1. V=Vendor. Mail the check directly to the vendor. Do not give cash.

If you are paying a power bill, send a check directly to the power company with the person's name and account number specified. Therefore you will know the money you are spending is used for the need you intended. Cash can easily be used for other expenses, things you would not want to support. You want to address a real need and not assist in the purchase of what might be harmful—maybe even deadly.

2. V=Verify. Verify the vendor or the story.

Call the power company. Talk with the landlord. People seeking help will often tell you what they believe you want to hear. This is not necessarily a con. It might simply be a way of establishing a relationship with you. A bottom line value for people who have lived in poverty for several generations is relationships. Their underlying belief might be, "If I tell you what I think you want to hear, you will like me. If you like me, you will help me." Ask for names of people you can call to verify the information and then follow through.

Suppose a man tells you that he needs food to feed his six children who are at home. Ask for their names and ages. If he stumbles with that information, he may be trying to stir your sympathy by telling you about children who don't exist. *Of course* you want to help children who you know with certainty exist and are hungry. *Of course* you do not want to give food to a man who will sell it on the street for drug money. You will feel better when you have checked the information, and you might learn information which encourages you to help even more—or not at all.

3. V=Voucher. Develop a voucher system for food and gas.

People often call congregations or show up at church offices with a request for food or gas for their car. They probably hope that the church will have a fund from which the pastor or secretary will give money for what they are seeking. Please do not give cash directly.

Obviously, you want to help people. If people are asking for food, address the need for food. There are several ways to do that. You might:

- Keep a food pantry in your building.
- Arrange a direct referral system to an existing food pantry located elsewhere in your community.
- Set up a voucher system with a restaurant, fast food place, or grocery store located in your vicinity. Set a limit on the cost of the meal.
- Purchase gift certificates to give.
- Specify that vouchers *cannot* be used to purchase alcohol, cigarettes, or any other specific items.

You can do the same for gasoline requests with a service station in your area. No system is perfect, but vouchers allow you to be sensitive to specific requests and still feel fairly confident that you did not inadvertently assist in destructive activities.

When you mail a payment directly to the *vendor*, *verify* the story, and use *vouchers*, you reduce the possibility of your gift of financial support being used for drugs or other illicit activities. By using the Three Vs (Vendor, Verify, and Voucher), you increase your wisdom while strengthening the effectiveness of your loving compassion.

The A-B-Cs of Helping

A third tool for discerning how to help is the A-B-Cs of Helping. This tool clarifies your conversations with people who are seeking help. The A-B-Cs will give you a framework for understanding why you may need to ask the same question in several different ways. They will help you stay connected without getting pulled into negative and destructive conversations.

*A=**A**cknowledge that the person does have a problem. Realize that people hear what they need to hear.*

Whenever anyone shares troubles with you, acknowledge that you heard what was said. You might say, "That really *is* a problem," or "That sounds difficult." You do not have to agree or disagree with the individual's own assessment of the situation. You simply acknowledge that you have heard what the person had to say. If you do *not* confirm that you have been present to the conversation, the requester will keep telling you his or her story over and over in a variety of ways. After all, each of us wants to know someone listened to us and heard what we had to say.

People will hear from you what they need to hear from you. That may not be what you actually said. For example, you might say that you will need to check with your mission coordinator about the possibility of helping this particular person. What the requester might hear is "After I talk with another person here at the church, we will help you." You indicate that you might or might not help. The person hears that help is on the way soon. When in crisis, all of us hold on to snippets of information which sound most like the words we want to hear.

What might sound like a lie to us is actually the person's recounting what he honestly believes he heard.

*B=Don't **B**elieve everything you hear.*

People usually do not intentionally lie. They tell you what they think you want to hear so that you will like them and thus help them. If you ask, "Are you a member of a church?" and the person perceives the correct answer is yes, she will respond, "Yes." She may or may not actually be connected with a congregation. She wants you to like her. Then you will help her. You may need to ask an important question in a variety of ways to get the most accurate information you need for making a decision. (Note: If a person says very negative things about a helping agency in your community, check out the comment directly with the agency. Learn the agency's policies and procedures so that you can evaluate for yourself the truth of the comments.)

*C=**C**hristianity (faith) is not judged by giving people exactly what they want.*

Occasionally when we say no, the person retorts, "I thought this was a Christian place!" When that happens, we can remind ourselves the word *no* is an equally caring and compassionate word. It does not help in the long term to continue to pay someone's bills without strongly encouraging him to begin doing things such as getting employment or furthering his education. In fact, paying someone's bills repeatedly, when she can and should be doing better, rewards her for handing responsibility for her life over to you rather than taking charge of her own situation.

We received a grant to hire some of our program participants as paid interns. We wanted to help them develop office skills and build work experience. One of the interns was especially engaging. She was full of enthusiasm, did whatever was asked of her, and encouraged the other interns and program participants along their journeys. She even earned the nickname "Fireball."

A full-time paid position became available. Fireball applied. Her direct supervisor encouraged her application and urged me to give her the job. However, I knew that the requirements and responsibilities of the situation were beyond Fireball's capabilities. I reluctantly told her that I was not going to offer her the position. She was furious with me, which I completely understood and accepted.

Several weeks later, Fireball appeared at my door and asked if I had a moment to speak with her. I assured her that of course I had time for her. She said, "You know, Beth, when you turned me down for that position, I was really angry with you."

I replied, "Yes, I know you were. It was not easy for me to say no to you."

Then she astounded me with "Your saying no to me was one of the best things that ever happened to me. It caused me to stop and look at myself and my situation. You were right. There are some other things which I need to pay attention to and work on right now." Even after all these years, Fireball stays in touch with me and lets me know how she is doing.

Remember:

> A=**A**cknowledge that the person does have a problem.
> Realize that people hear what they need to hear.
> B=Don't **B**elieve everything you hear.
> C=**C**hristianity (faith) is not judged by giving people exactly what they want.

L.E.A.R.N.

A fourth tool is L.E.A.R.N. how to say no. There are times when you must say no. You might believe that no is the best response now for the person who is requesting your help. You may have policies about when, who, and how to help that prevent you from saying yes at the moment. You simply may not have the resources available to offer assistance.

You can learn to say no in loving, firm, and compassionate ways. Using L.E.A.R.N. can help you say no in ways which may even result in a hug afterward because you cared!

L=Learn the available resources.

Learn about the agencies in your community and what services they offer. There may be people in your congregation who work or volunteer at organizations that offer significant help to people in need. Social workers at hospitals and in schools often know the resources available. United Ways may be a good source of information about community services.

E=Explain the reasoning behind your answer.

Don't apologize when you say no. You have nothing to apologize for. You are following the guidelines developed by the mission committee or the congregation as a whole. You might say, "Our congregation's policy is that we do not help with that particular need," or "We do not help people who come without a referral from one of our partner agencies." You can say this with compassion and yet with firmness. People tend to accept your decision and do not argue when they understand the "why" of your refusal.

One side note: There is great power in the words you choose. Whenever you say, "I won't help you," you are operating from a place of strength. You are operating from a well-thought-out process of compassion and servant ministry. When you say, "I can't help you," the other person might hear, "You *could* help me if you wanted to." With "I can't," you are opening the door for arguments.

A=**A**sk only appropriate questions.

You may be very curious about many things in a person's life. However, ask only questions that assist you in deciding whether you will help or not. Sometimes volunteers in United Ministries' Emergency Assistance program want to know why the children in a family all have different last names. That is not information we need to determine whether we will pay a heating bill.

R=**R**eferrals …make good ones.

When you learn what other organizations in your community offer people in need, be careful about interpreting their policies and programs to someone else. Agencies cease offering certain services due to loss of funding or personnel. A program may no longer fit their mission. Do not tell people who are already in distress to go elsewhere unless you are absolutely sure the other organization can and will help. Folks seeking help definitely do not need to spend their limited resources on transportation or walk a long distance only to discover they were sent yet one more time to ask for things that don't exist or for which they don't qualify.

N=**N**ever explain another organization's policies unless you're positive about your information.

Agency policies can change. *Never* say, "Go to Agency X. They will help you." The better thing to say is: "Agency X may be able to help you. You might check with them." Knowing that people hear what they need to hear, the person seeking assistance may still hear that Agency X will help them, but you know that you gave assistance without promising something you cannot make happen.

Your goal when you say no is to provide the best help you can at the present moment for the present situation. To help you remain connected with the person seeking assistance, even when you give the answer you know he or she does not want to hear, remember:

> *L=**L**earn the available resources.*
> *E=**E**xplain the reasoning behind your answer.*
> *A=**A**sk only appropriate questions.*
> *R=**R**eferrals ... make good ones.*
> *N=**N**ever explain another organization's policies unless*
> *you're positive about your information.*

Double Standards

Earlier in this chapter, we talked about the cultural differences between people with resources and people without resources. As we think about the techniques we can use to ensure we are servants rather than suckers, we also need to consider the double standards that influence our desires to help.

We look at the world through our own lenses. We approach solutions to issues of poverty based on our gender, educational level, geographic area, age, socioeconomic level, and health. We also see faults and failures of another person without realizing that we, too, may be guilty of those same things. For example, we get angry when people won't go to budgeting class to improve their financial situation. Yet we don't go to the gym even though we know we need to exercise regularly to improve our health.

We both know what we need to do, but neither of us does what is necessary. The specifics of our "shortcomings" may be different. Nevertheless, the issues are the same. (We are not paying attention to our health, whether financial or physical!) Thus we have double standards. To use a metaphor from the Bible, we see the speck in our neighbor's eye and cannot see the log in our own.

Let's look at a few of the inconsistencies we exhibit when we look at people who are poor as compared to our own situations. As you consider these double standards, which ones anger you, which are a discovery to you, and which are completely correct?

1. Double Standard: "Poor people who stay home with their children are 'lazy.' I applaud my friends who stay home with their kids because they provide consistent, loving, and quality childcare."

Some government assistance programs require the recipient to work in the community. (The opportunities for meeting the requirements vary state by state.) However, when requirements for work are yoked with receiving financial assistance, child care becomes a challenge. There are not enough child care subsidies to go around. Child care is often expensive or, if affordable, may be of poor quality. When a father or mother who lives in poverty chooses to stay home with young children, we often label him or her as lazy. When someone we know who may be in our socioeconomic class chooses to stay home, we applaud her for her commitment to her family or cheer him for being so involved with his children. This is a double standard.

2. Double Standard: "People should not need government services. So what if I use parks, public school systems, and transportation services?"

Government services which benefit people who live in poverty are often targets for cuts by legislators. The people who are most affected by these sometimes draconian measures are the least likely to be active constituents or voters. However, we all receive government services, either directly through our jobs (public school teachers, as one example), or we use public parks, airports, etc. Usually when people talk about cutting government services, they are talking about the services that benefit "those people." We challenge anyone to touch the services that benefit "me and mine."

One service benefiting "me and mine" is the ability to write off from our taxes the interest we pay on our mortgages. Government-supported housing continues to be in a downward trend. (For ongoing updates about what is happening in low-income housing, visit www.nlihc.org, the Web site of the National Low Income Housing Coalition.) There is no community in this entire nation where an individual earning minimum wage can adequately afford a rental unit at the fair market rate.

However, those of us who have mortgages on our homes receive a tremendous indirect governmental subsidy, a "tax break," when we deduct our mortgage interest on our federal income taxes. According to the Congressional Joint Committee on Taxation, the tax breaks for mortgage interests totaled $70.1 billion in 2004. [12] The double standard becomes apparent when we realize that the government subsidizes luxury items such as boats, cars, and second homes—paid for with equity loans—and yet continues to reduce funding for public housing and housing vouchers.

3. Double Standard: *"Poor people should spend only on the necessities, but 'splurging' or treating myself is okay. I deserve it."*

Remember: the bottom-line values for people in generational poverty are entertainment and relationships. Therefore, when money is available, spending it on entertainment may be the priority. Who doesn't want a treat after being deprived for a time?

A former employee at United Ministries grew up financially poor. She said that she owed the utility company money. She could not remember the exact amount of the bill but guessed that it was about $100. She said, "I called the company and told them that I had $50 to pay on my bill. They said they needed $100. I told them that I did not have $100, but I had $50 which I was willing to give them. They said, 'No, we need $100.'" She further explained, "I tried to give them the money, but they wouldn't take it. I went out and took my $50 and bought me some new clothes!" She *tried* to give them the money. When they refused to take it, she treated herself!

4. Double Standard: *"If people would stay in school, they would succeed. I did!"*

Staying in school does not guarantee success, though it does greatly enhance it. Through United Ministries' Emergency Assistance program, we have paid the bill to reconnect electricity for teachers with master's degrees. We have assisted in restoring water to a home where both adults had college educations. Through the Place of Hope, our day shelter for people who are homeless, we have worked with former attorneys who lost everything due to drugs or mental illness.

Nevertheless, we all know that education does improve our choices and options.

Today teachers are not necessarily the same race, culture, or socioeconomic group as their students. As important as racial differences are, the more important difference is socioeconomic. We absorb our vocabulary and values from our socioeconomic class. We learn subtle ... and not so subtle ... ways of thinking and behaving from our socioeconomic class.

Many teachers are middle class. They are challenged by students in their classrooms who come from poverty. Here is one illustration of what public school teachers learn from a workshop I lead for them: Students who come from overcrowded situations may be afraid of silence. Quiet often means in their world that something uncomfortable or scary is about to happen. On the other hand, teachers require quiet in the classroom for desk work. Once teachers learn that their pupils may be unable to concentrate on their work when the room is silent, they design ways to reduce the child's anxiety. They may play soft music, for example.

5. *Double Standard: "If poor people would leave their families, get new friends, move from their bad neighborhoods, learn new patterns of thinking, and develop new ways of relating to others, then their lives could improve." And then we ask, "How easy is it for us to do these things?"*

Some years ago, United Ministries began a program called the Magdalene Project for women meeting two of these four criteria: homeless, pregnant, a prostitute, or addicted. I met weekly with the women to discuss a variety of issues: relationships, health, men, addiction, children, and personal issues. Because the staff and committed volunteers were willing to be in significant relationships with the women, to become their best friends and their worst enemies, and to give hugs or kicks in the rear end as needed, some of the women began to change their lives significantly. We helped them into addiction and/or mental health treatment, legitimate employment, prenatal care if they were pregnant, and new ways of thinking.

As we learned more and more of their stories, we realized some of the women needed to leave their families (family members were their drug dealers or pimps), move from their bad neighborhoods (where drugs and violence were prevalent), learn new patterns of thinking (each person was valuable), and develop new ways of relating to others (foul language and bad attitudes do not often get you what you want). These tasks were huge, and yet some of the women were able to make the bold changes required.

When I realized what was being asked of the Magdalene women and the others in the various programs at United Ministries, I acknowledged the astounding fact that people were *indeed* changing their lives—even with unbelievable obstacles facing them. I recognized that *I* might not be able to do all the tasks required for the kind of life changes these women were working toward.

Are you willing to leave your family? Can you move from your neighborhood where everything is familiar? Will you learn new patterns of thinking? Ever tried to break just one habit? Are you able to develop new ways of relating to others? These tasks can seem insurmountable and yet are often essential for redirection to happen. No wonder permanent change can be very difficult.

6. *Double Standard: "Those people just choose their lives. Sure they may have grown up in a bad environment, but that's no excuse. I pulled myself up. They can, too."*

The family in which we grow up affects the options we have available in our lives. Most of us reading this book can choose where we will live, which doctor we will go to, where we can shop, and what kind of car we will drive. We are not forced to live only where the rents are lowest, to use only whatever health clinic doctor is on duty, or to use only stores to which we can walk. These kinds of stores often have poor quality product and charge high prices because they have a captive clientele: only people in the immediate vicinity!

A donor I know truly believed that because he had overcome his childhood situation, anyone could. One day he came to my office and handed me a check. Then he quipped, "I don't know why you help these people." I was genuinely puzzled since he had just made a substantial contribution. I asked him to sit down so we could talk. I discovered he was a self-made man and supported many charities. He had grown up on a farm, was the first in his family to graduate from high school, and the first to make his way in the world. He ended his story with "If I can do it, anyone can." The conversation ended. I thanked him profusely for his gift, and he left.

I continued to consider his assertion, "If I can do it, anyone can." If I were to have that conversation again, I would continue our dialogue and explain that growing up on a farm taught him the very valuable lesson of "cause and effect." He learned that if he wanted to harvest, he had to plow and to plant. Many of the people I've worked with have not had the opportunity to learn about cause and effect.

Then I would illustrate my point. "Suppose one morning a child gets up and goes into the kitchen where Mom hugs and kisses the child and says, 'You are the cutest child. I just love you to death!' The second morning the child gets up, walks into the kitchen, and Mom hits the child in the head, so hard the child slams into the wall. On the third morning, the child gets up, goes into the kitchen, and *if* Mom is there, she totally ignores her child. If that is the kind of environment you grow up in, you may not understand cause and effect."

If a person does not understand cause and effect, success on the job may be challenging because cause and effect is a foundation of the world of work. An employee may not understand that he or she cannot say more than once, "That's not in my job description," and expect to keep the job.

What family we're born into does make a difference in how we view the world, in the lessons we learn, and in the skills we develop for successful and healthy lives. Our family of origin affects the choices we have—both the quantity and quality of our decisions.

7. Double Standard: "Anyone can get a job if they want one. Of course, I do have transportation, child care, contacts in the community, adequate people skills, and good health."

When people say, "Anybody could get a job if they wanted one," they usually follow with something such as "I would flip hamburgers if my family needed me to do that." This comment indicates the person speaking has little regard for hamburger-flipping jobs and thinks those jobs are demeaning! Those jobs *are* typically low paying, without benefits, and inconsistent when and how many hours are offered. The job counselors at United Ministries *will* help someone find a "hamburger flipping" job *if* he needs immediate income or *if* she has a bad work history or no work history. "Hamburger flipping" jobs simply help a person stay in the current situation. Such jobs generally do not help someone progress.

Many of the people who come to United Ministries have indeed worked at "hamburger flipping" jobs. They want more but have barriers to overcome. Getting and keeping a job is more than simply a strong desire to work. One also needs the infrastructure of transportation, people skills, adequate health, and childcare to be employed.

Servant or Sucker?

We truly want to help. We desire to be servants, not suckers. Nevertheless, we are suckers when we react without thought, when we give for unworthy reasons, and when we believe *yes* is the only caring word. We are less likely to be suckers when we understand the socioeconomic values of the people we are trying to serve. We are servants when we realize that solutions that make sense to us (because of our own way of seeing the world based on our education, gender, or socioeconomic situation) may not be good for other people. We are servants when we enter caring relationships with others whether those relationships are short, as through eye contact, or extend over a longer time.

We want to help. We want to serve. We can use the mantras, the three Vs, the A-B-Cs of helping, and L.E.A.R.N. to improve our skills of discernment when we reach out to people in poverty. We can pay attention to how we are blind to other people's realities as we consider our double standards. When we become more thoughtful in helping people in poverty, we will be servants…not suckers!

Questions to Consider

1. Will these insights change how you or your group reaches out to people in need? If so, how?

2. Is any information in this chapter applicable to your work, school, or family situation? If so, how?

3. If this material reminds you of a time when you thought you were helping but now realize you didn't, how would you currently handle a similar situation?

4. Which of the double standards sounded uncomfortably familiar to you? Why?

5. Do you disagree with any of the double standards? Which one(s)? Why?

6. What is the most important insight you gained from this chapter? Why?

Exercise

Helping Agency XYZ Application [13]

We as a society often ask people to do what they cannot do. They cannot read. They do not understand our words. They have no framework for grasping what we are saying or explaining. When asked a question, they answer with what they think we're looking for so that we will like them and help them. Their answer may not be accurate for the information we seek.

This exercise allows us to experience the frustration of not being able to do something important when requested to do it. The "application" makes us aware of the need to explore varieties of ways of communication with people we care about and want to help.

Prior to looking at the application, please follow these instructions:

Before you turn the page for the application, understand that you are applying for services at Helping Agency XYZ. You must answer every question. If you do not answer every question, you will not receive any services. Furthermore, even if you answer every question, if the interviewer doesn't like one of your answers, *or* if we discover that you lied, not only will you not receive services at Agency XYZ, you will not receive services anywhere in this community. Now complete the application.

STOP NOW and complete the application before proceeding.
(Allow yourself adequate time to get frustrated.)

Helping Agency XYZ Application

Praenomen:

Cognomen:

Address:

1. Were you ever rusticated?   ____yes ____ no

2. Have you ever had to miss work due to:
   Accouchement?   ____yes ____ no
   Contagion?   ____yes ____ no

3. Would you describe yourself as being:
   Vituperative?   ____yes ____ no
   Assiduous?   ____yes ____ no
   Acrimonious?   ____yes ____ no

4. Have you ever been accused of:
   Peculation?   ____yes ____ no
   Catachresis?   ____yes ____ no

Of course this is not a real application. Ask yourself, "If this *were* a real application, how would you have handled it?" Your answers might include:

- "I'd ask for help." (Note: This response requires a certain level of self-esteem. Many people will not admit they cannot do what you've asked them to do.)
- "I just remembered that I have an appointment. Can I bring this back to you tomorrow?" (Note:

This response allows for someone else to complete the application for the program participant.)

- "These are not my reading glasses. Can I bring this back tomorrow?" (Note: Same as previous response.)
- "I'd just check the boxes and hope I did the right ones." (Note: How many times have you done this on a test for which you were ill prepared?)
- "I'd get an attitude and storm out of the room." (Note: Fear of being found inadequate can produce anger. Anger is a very strong defense mechanism. We see this behavior when someone cannot complete a job application in the employment workshop. Rather than ask for help, the person "develops an attitude" and storms out of the room.)

Because relationship is often a bottom line value, a person might give the answer he or she believes the questioner is looking for. The belief is "If you like me, you will help me." As a society we often ask people to do things they literally cannot do. We might have to ask an important question in several different ways to get the information we really need. *Most* people are not trying to con us, but that does not mean that they will give the most accurate information when we first ask.

By experiencing the challenges of this exercise, you now have a sense of what people who are seeking your help may feel. You can be patient and understanding as you ask a question in a variety of ways because you realize that the person is not deliberately being contrary. He simply does not understand what you are asking. She wants to make you happy by giving you the answers you want. Neither is trying to lie. They both just want help. Remembering your own brief sense of frustration of trying to do something you literally could not do can help you connect on a feeling level as you begin to reach out with love and care.

Exercise Questions to Consider

1. Do you have a personal illustration for asking (or being asked) to do something without the capability to do it?

2. Now that you have done this exercise, will your behavior change? If so, in what way?

In Case You're Interested: Definitions

Accouchement	Going to or being put to bed
Acrimonious	Bitingly hostile in language or tone
Assiduous	Diligent
Catachresis	Strained use of a word or phrase
Cognomen	Surname, family name
Contagion	Transmittable disease
Peculation	Embezzlement of money
Praenomen	First or given name
Rusticated	Having been sent to the country
Vituperative	Harshly abusive

Chapter Eight
Different Approaches for Offering Assistance

C HURCH MEMBERS OFTEN STRUGGLE to know the best way *for them and their congregation* to fulfill Jesus' mandate of serving people who are poor or in crisis. They sincerely want to help but question whether the way they are providing financial assistance is truly the most Christian way for them as well as for the people who receive their help.

Every approach along a continuum of styles has both benefits and problems. It is up to the leaders and clergy of the congregation to decide which one suits best their understanding of their mission, their staff's skills, and their understanding of God.

We will consider each of these approaches in helping people who are in crisis.

Responding to Anyone at Any Time

People may come to the church anytime there appears to be a member or staff person in the building or in the parking lot. It may be during weekday office hours. It may be right before a big wedding. It may be as the youth group is gathering for their overnight lock-in. People also call the church, the secretary, the pastor, or the missions committee chairperson and ask for assistance. No matter when someone shows up requesting help, a member or staff person talks with him or her and responds appropriately.

Pros

Some congregations believe that being present whenever someone seeks help is the loving and caring thing to do. Jesus commands us to feed the hungry, clothe the naked, etc. Members honestly believe that it is not their place to make judgments about who does and who does not get help.

This biblically grounded thought needs to be considered in the context of the congregation's theology and sense of mission as the leaders decide how best to serve others. They know the congregation has the resources needed. A loving church is obliged to support whoever requests it, whenever the request is made —within reason.

Some congregations know that their members live lives that afford them little contact with people who are poor and so choose to provide an opportunity for engagement within their walls. When congregations welcome anyone in need into the church, they are welcoming Jesus Christ himself.

Cons

There are concerns with this approach. Often the person who responds to the person requesting assistance is the church pastor or secretary. He or she may be busy doing other necessary tasks of the church (writing sermons, providing pastoral counseling, visiting shut-ins, mailing the newsletter, copying materials for the Deacons meeting, etc.) and may not have time to spend with the person who is seeking assistance. The choices then become:

a. Stop doing the other work which the congregation requires and spend whatever time the person needs in order to be treated as a valued child of God.

b. Give the person something just so he/she will leave.

c. Ask the person to sit and wait … and wait … until the pastor returns to the building, the task is completed, or the lay person designated to handle such requests arrives.

The person seeking assistance may be in real need. He or she may indeed have a prescription for a sick child. He or she may truly need help with a rent bill. On the other hand, he or she may be seeking cash or some item that can be sold on the street for illegal drug money. When the cash will be used to purchase drugs, the church does not reinforce the blessedness of the person as a beloved child of God but actually helps the person's journey to self-inflicted death.

Safety can become an issue with this approach, especially if the only person in the building is a lone female. The people coming in with requests *may* have mental-illness or drug-abuse issues that can lead to violence.

Even when everything works smoothly in receiving the request, responding appropriately to the request, and affirming the person's worthiness as a child of God, there can still be a gap in this approach. The person may leave with a bag of food or the assurance that the church will pay the bill—and nothing else. No one offered in-depth questioning or a follow-up meeting to discern issues in the person's life that, if addressed, could lead to significant future growth. The requester leaves with a momentary solution to the problem but no hope of a long-term solution. No one offers plans or programs to assure that the person can meet his or her responsibilities without having to be dependent on the charitable gifts of congregations or agencies.

Setting Appointments

By setting appointments, the minister, mission director, or trained volunteer picks a specific time to meet with people who are seeking assistance. A church may decide, for example, that on Thursday mornings the minister will set aside time for people who are asking for help. Anyone who walks in or calls for aid at other times will be given a Thursday morning appointment. On the appointment day, the minister or person designated to meet with the requester will be able to focus completely on the individual who is hurting. There are similarities both pro and con with the first option of responding to anyone at any time.

Pros

Setting appointments helps address the issue of people coming in for quick money for a quick drug fix. Requiring someone to return for an appointment often means that those who *do* return have a legitimate, verifiable need.

People who spend quality time with folks in need will feel pleasure at being able to help someone. The interviewer's own spiritual journey will be enriched because of the connection with someone Jesus most certainly would have spent time with.

Cons

Lack of follow-up may still be an issue. The interviewer may or may not know of other resources in the community that could offer the requester long-term solutions to his/her situation. Without knowledge about programs for assistance with employment, adult education, financial management, and/or medical concerns *and* without strong and intentional follow-up, the requester may not access further growth opportunities.

Assisting Only Referrals

Congregations can choose to help with financial assistance by entering formal or informal agreements with helping agencies in their communities. The agency provides the basic screening of the person making the request, and the church pays the bill when receiving a referral or request from the agency.

Pros

Some congregations want to help directly from their church facility but know that no one there is equipped to make decisions about whom to help, how much to help, and when to help. They choose to respond by requiring that a person be referred by an established helping agency. A referral from a professional agency person provides a sense that the requester has been screened and is eligible for the church's assistance.

Some congregations require the requester to come to the church to receive the help. Others require only a phone call from a caseworker in a referring agency, after which a check is written to the vendor providing the service (landlord, utility company, etc.).

Cons

The downside of this approach is that members of the congregation may feel that they have moved to a more "hands-off" approach than with any of the previous options discussed.

Directing Requests to an Appropriate Organization

The congregation may choose to direct anyone requesting assistance to an organization supported financially by the church. No requests are addressed directly at the church.

Pros

Some congregations know that they do not have the qualifications or time to make good decisions about helping people on a case-by-case basis. They give all their crisis assistance money to an organization with which they have a relationship or a formalized partnership for service. The church understands that the helping organization is an extension of their service ministry and that they are partners in reaching out to others.

The intentions of the decision makers in the congregation to help through a partner agency are based on the belief that by giving funds to an organization totally equipped to work with people in need, the congregation may be offering not only short-term help but also long-term solutions.

For example, when a person is told by a congregation's staff member or volunteer to go to Agency RST, the organization can use the opportunity of the person's request for rent or utilities assistance to encourage him or her to access other programs within the organization. These programs may involve training for employment, obtaining additional education, developing parenting skills, confronting addictions, etc. The trained volunteers or staff people within Agency RST may covenant with the individual to continue a working partnership for a week, a month, or even a year. Getting connected with a strong, helping organization may be the best and most holy thing that ever happened to those who are motivated to change their lives in a positive way.

Cons

This way of assisting people may feel removed from members of the congregation, as if they're not really caring. Members may perceive this option as a very "hands-off" approach.

Congregations who want their members to have the opportunity for direct contact with people who are poor can encourage members to volunteer in Agency RST. The interaction between the congregation's members and the Agency RST staff and participants can enrich the sense of God's love and compassion for everyone.

Creating a Fully Staffed Program Within the Church

A congregation may believe their understanding of mission requires them to hire staff whose role is to provide assistance to members and to needy people in the community. Pros and cons from previous options may also apply here.

Pros

Having trained people, both paid and volunteer, with skills for interviewing, assessing the real situation, and suggesting long-term solutions to financial need is a benefit of an on-site crisis ministry. The members and staff fulfill their own sense of ministry by meeting and interacting with people in poverty and by helping them as they are able.

The congregation visibly lives out the gospel mandate of caring for people in need. The church develops the reputation of being a loving and caring congregation. Worship services, education classes, and youth gatherings can highlight the needs of the people who seek assistance. The church can use real-life examples when it educates its members about mercy, justice, and *shalom*.

Cons

There are two drawbacks to having an on-site crisis ministry program. The first is the expense of paid staff—part-time or full-time—to train and supervise the volunteers, to fill in when volunteers are unavailable, and to provide backup for situations that may become difficult to handle.

The second concern is that the congregation may be seduced into satisfaction with its charity work and never move to justice work. When offering charity, the giver can decide when to stop. Charity helps deal with the immediate crisis but offers no process for working on the deeper issues...those life happenings that force someone to seek financial assistance. Justice is about working for *shalom*, that sense of the kingdom of God where everyone has what is needed to become fully the person God created him or her to be.

Both charity work and justice work are vital and important. Offering a soup kitchen, as essential as that is, without asking, "Why can't this person afford a meal?" is stopping two stops too early on the train ride to the kingdom of God. Justice work requires asking, "Does this person need the meal at the soup kitchen because of lack of a job, lack of training for that job, inequitable wages for the work performed, etc.?" If the answer is yes to that questioning analysis, the congregation may decide to do what is possible to address that imbalance.

The congregation may honestly claim that its mission in its community is charity work. This call is sacred and is to be honored. However the congregation needs to acknowledge that it is appropriate to ask other questions and address other concerns—and if they don't do so, perhaps someone else must.

Partnering with Others in Your Community

In a number of communities, congregations and faith groups have come together to form an organization which is termed *cooperative ministry*. These service ministries often begin as a way to collectively and compassionately handle all the requests received by ministers, church secretaries, and mission leaders. By establishing cooperative ministries, congregational leaders know they are helping in significant ways without constant interruptions. They also reduce "church hopping"—the pattern where someone receives help from multiple churches in multiple ways.

Pros

Cooperative ministries may hand out food and clothing, pay rent or utility bills, and respond to perceived needs. As cooperative ministries mature and become solidly established, they may move beyond the Band-Aid mentality of providing basic necessities and create a process of addressing the reasons *why* people need help. At that point in their development, they may establish employment training programs, adult education classes, housing ventures, intense case management and counseling, addiction services, leadership training, and a host of other programs specific to their community's needs.

Some cooperative ministries remain extensions of the supporting congregations' service ministries. Others move away from their roots in the faith community. Some cooperative ministries are highly evangelistic in their approaches, requiring attendance at worship services in order to receive assistance, while others tend to speak about issues of faith only when asked by the program participants to do so. Cooperative ministries may enjoy the support of an array of denomination and faith perspectives in addition to other sources such as government grants, foundation support, and United Way funding. Some are Christian; others are ecumenical with non-Christian as well as Christian support; and still others are interfaith when they bring Muslims, Buddhists, Hindus, Jews, and Christians together to address human need.

Cooperative ministries are often a logical partner for a congregation to choose in their efforts in serving others.

Cons

The cooperative ministry's mission may not align with yours. If you choose to partner with an existing cooperative ministry in your area, learn what the organization's mission is. Make sure that the approach of the cooperative ministry is compatible with your congregation's understanding of ministry and mission.

Ask questions about what the board of directors and staff mean in the organization's mission statement and how it fulfills its goals. Learn the scope and requirements of the cooperative ministry's programs. Ask if someone can notify you through an e-mail alert about scams when people are "church hopping" (seeking assistance at church after church) or when people are especially threatening in their approach or request.

Determine how you might support the cooperative ministry: financially, with volunteers, by hosting an event, or in other ways. Find out what services the cooperative ministry might be able to provide for you. Does the organization offer direct services with people requesting money, workshops or training, advocacy programs, etc.?

There are other organizations in many communities which can partner with you in helping people in need. Search these out, and find ways that you, your congregation, and the community organization can work together to solve problems with individuals and in the community as a whole.

Note: Chapter 11 will help the leadership of your congregation develop a process for deciding which agencies, ministries, and organizations to support.

Choosing Any Combination of the Above

Finally, congregations may choose to use only one or a combination of these different ways of ministering to people in financial need. Each congregation needs to explore which strategy best meets its mission and its situation.

Any of these approaches can be enriched by building a strong relationship with other organizations in the community that also offer assistance. When members and volunteers know helping agency people who will work alongside them, they can call for advice when facing a challenging decision, for information about someone who may be "church hopping," or for help paying an individual's large bill.

We all want to help. We want to help in God's way. We pray for discernment about what that means for each congregation and each person who needs our help. We will seek the best way(s) for our congregation to be a loving neighbor to people in need.

Different Approaches for Offering Assistance

Approach	Pros	Cons
Responding to anyone at any time	Loving and caring congregation Non-judgmental Opportunity to interact	Untimely interruptions Help given for wrong reasons Person may wait to be seen No follow-up Safety issues Lack of screening
Setting Appointments	Keeping appointment means higher probability of real need Chance to begin relationship	Lack of follow-up Lack of referral information
Assisting Only Referrals	Screening is done by pros	Less "hands-on"
Directing Requests to an Appropriate Agency	Agency is equipped and trained Extends service ministry	Feels "removed"
Creating a Fully Staffed Program Within the Church	Assessment and intervention Visible hands-on ministry Members can interact	Expensive Charity rather than justice
Partnering with Others in Your Community	Cooperative ministry model Active and hands-on partner Reduces "church hopping" More holistic solutions Volunteer opportunities	Misalignment of mission

Questions to Consider

1. If you are a member of a congregation that provides direct service to people in need, which description best fits your circumstance?

2. Which way of reaching out is most appealing to you? Why?

3. Are there reasons to consider choosing one option over another within your congregation?

4. Do you agree or disagree with the strengths and weaknesses of each option for helping? Why or why not?

Chapter Nine
Setting up a Direct Aid Ministry

YOU AND LEADERS OF your congregation may decide that it is now time for the congregation to begin reaching beyond its own doors to help others in the community. At this point, you decide to develop a direct aid ministry. You are not sure in what ways you want to reach out directly. You only know that God has placed a desire in your heart to do something. How do you start?

By working through a deliberative process, you can help ensure the success of your new program as well as prevent some of the potential problems in such a ministry. There are no right answers to the questions. There are only valuable answers in making sure that everyone understands and accepts the privileges and responsibilities of a direct aid ministry.

Exploring the "Itch"

Consider the reasons you believe it is time to begin a direct aid ministry in your congregation.

Note: A worksheet of the questions is at the end of this chapter.

1. Why do you want to do this?

People choose to be involved in a direct aid ministry for all kinds of reasons. Some of those motivations are very faithful. Some are not.

Others are somewhere in between. Ask yourself and each other why you are choosing to be part of this process.

- Were you or your family helped by someone in the past?
- Do you believe this is what people of faith do?
- Do you believe that your congregation is self-absorbed and needs to reach out?
- Are you in an area of high need?
- Do you live or work in an affluent area, and you want to reach out to others who have more limited resources?
- Have you worked in human services, and now you want your congregation to be engaged with you?
- Why do you want to do direct aid ministry?

Remember, there are no right answers, only valuable answers.

2. Are there other groups in your area doing similar things?

There are many needs in any community. If another group is already focusing on the area you are considering, you may choose to look for another need. On the other hand, the issue may be so large that more hands, hearts, and heads working on the particular concern is important.

3. Is there a need for services in your area?

Can you measure the specific need through hard data, anecdotal evidence, or personal interviews with people who can help quantify the need that is not being met in any other way? Are you sure your passion matches up with a community need?

4. Are there enough people interested in this project to plan and carry it out?

Before you begin direct aid ministry, think about who in the congregation may be a candidate for taking part in this ministry. Are there enough people interested in this project to support the planning and implementation effort? As few as one or two people who share a passion for direct aid can be the catalysts the congregation needs to venture forth. On the other hand, only one or two people may quickly feel overwhelmed by the demands and challenges of developing and offering a direct aid ministry. Are there enough people? Only you can define "enough" for your particular situation.

5. *Who else wants to do this?*

Hopefully there are other people in the congregation who, upon learning that a group is considering a direct aid ministry, will share the small group's passion for direct aid ministry, however it might be defined. Who are they? How will they know that there is a potential ministry opportunity for them? How and when will you engage them in the process, or *will* you involve others at this point?

6. *Is there another organization with whom you could partner?*

Seek out others in your community who may be doing what you are proposing. Is there a demonstrated need for you and them to do the exact same thing? Are there ways in which you can complement each other? Are you offering the same services but for different beneficiary groups? If another community organization is doing very effective direct aid ministry for the need you have identified, you may consider partnering with it rather than beginning something on your own. One simple benefit could be to develop a system for referring program participants directly back and forth. When two groups work together, you may be able to accomplish more with better efficiency and increased effectiveness.

If partnering is not appealing, you can certainly learn from the other organization's successes and setbacks. They may be willing to offer expert advice and guidance as you plan your direct aid ministry. They may be willing to give you information about certain people from their database—within confidentiality guidelines, of course.

7. Do you have support from the church leadership to explore this kind of ministry?

It can be disheartening for a small group of members to plan a great direct aid ministry with enthusiasm only to discover the leadership of the congregation does not support this new venture. Ask who you need to approach about your intentions for a direct aid ministry, and then seek their approval to explore your options. Assure the leaders that you will seek final approval for a direct aid ministry when appropriate, but for now you want the nod to proceed conceptually.

Now you have completed your assessment of why direct service ministry is important for you and your congregation. You have made the decision to proceed. The next step is to decide how to begin.

Whom/How/When to serve

The needs are great, and your resources of time and talent are limited. Now you will define your focus for your direct aid ministry. You want to have strong impact on the needs you plan to address.

1. Who is your target group?

After you've ascertained that you want to proceed with planning a direct aid ministry, you begin the part which is often fun, yet challenging.

> Whom do you want to serve?
> How do you want to serve?
> When and how frequently do you want to serve?
> Who is your target group?
> Do you want to serve only senior citizens?
> Only children?
> Only adolescents?
> What age(s) are the people to whom you want to reach out?
> Is it important that you serve only women or female-headed households?
> Do you want to serve only single fathers?

Do you want to help only widows?

Do you want any gender limitations for your target group?

Is there a specific geographic area that you want to serve? For example, do you want to focus on a one-mile radius of your worship center?

Do you want to limit to a certain neighborhood or zip code?

Shall you help people who live somewhere in your county?

In your state?

In your region?

Is the help you are considering only for members of your congregation or for people who worship with you regularly?

Do the people need to profess your faith?

There are no right answers, only valuable ones, as you begin to clarify your vision for your direct aid ministry.

2. What services do you want to provide?

Do you want to offer financial assistance with rent, utilities, or prescription medications? Do you want to provide food bags or a hot meal? Do you want to provide social gathering opportunities? Do you want to provide child care?

The kinds of things you offer through your direct aid ministry are limited only by your own vision and resources. For example, United Ministries in Greenville, South Carolina, grew a number of programs out of lessons learned from people who came to its Emergency Assistance program, which gives food bags in addition to financial help with rent, utilities, heat, and prescriptions. Because homeless people regularly stopped by asking for help, United Ministries opened the Place of Hope, a day shelter with hot showers, a message center, telephone, mailing address, washers and dryers, and assistance with mental illness, addictions, and long-term housing. United Ministries realized that people needed help with employment skills and getting jobs. It created the Employment Readiness program to help people find and keep employment. A huge barrier to employment was lack of education; therefore, the Adult Education program was added to help people earn their GED.

The needs are boundless. You can discern where your skills, gifts, interests, energy, and love are leading you for direct aid. There will be someone or a group of people who will greatly benefit from what you have to offer.

3. How often may a household receive services?

If you decide to offer "things"—food bags, meals, financial assistance, clothing, shelter, etc.—you will need to determine how frequently you will provide assistance to a household. Will the family be eligible for a food bag weekly? Monthly? Every three months? Every six months? Be able to explain your rationale for your decisions. For example, United Ministries helps a household with rent or utilities only once in a twelve-month period. The reason is that the organization interviews about 500 households a month *and* because it offers more than bill payment. United Ministries provides job placement assistance and education opportunities, thereby freeing a family to meet its needs without having to ask for assistance. On the other hand, homeless people can shower every day the Place of Hope is open because they need access to those services.

4. What is your intake process?

What questions will you ask of the people who seek help from you? Some groups choose to ask no questions and give simply because someone asks. Other groups ask for name, address, Social Security number, contact phone number, names and birth dates of everyone in the household, income by category (earned, food stamps, disability, social security, veteran benefits, etc.), and expenses by category (rent, lights, heat, phone, transportation, medical, etc.). As you develop your intake form, make sure that all the questions are truly relevant to your decision-making process for providing assistance and not simply curiosity questions. Think about how you would feel if you were asked the questions you include, and then ask only the essential ones. Decide if your intake form is only on paper, only in the computer, or both.

5. When will you offer services?

If you are running a clothing closet, for example, you may decide to open every Saturday morning or only once a month. If you are choosing to provide financial assistance, will it be available any time the doors of the worship center are open? One morning a week? When? Some congregations have found that taking appointments for a specific morning helps discourage people who are looking for a quick handout. Those who keep the appointment are more likely to truly need your assistance. If you are having a social gathering for neighborhood residents, you may offer it monthly or quarterly.

Note: Chapter 8 discusses different approaches for offering help.

6. How will you provide payment for bills, if
you decide to help in that way?

Bills should always be paid directly to the vendor (landlord, utility company, pharmacy, etc.) Never give the money directly to the person you are helping. Who in the congregation will actually write the checks? What authorization will be followed? If a payment needs to happen before the regular check-writing time, what is the process for expediting?

7. What is your budget?

When beginning a direct aid ministry, budgets and money are necessary considerations. How much money will this program require? Some congregations use only the funds provided by special offerings. Others write specific amounts into their budget. Still others call individual members within the congregation with targeted requests.

One way to develop your budget is to decide the maximum amount of financial assistance you will provide per household and then determine how many households you want to help each month. For example, if you choose to help households with rent, you could decide to give a maximum of $75. You decide to help a maximum of twenty families a month. Seventy-five times twenty equals $1,500 a month. Therefore the budget needs $1,500 a month. Or if the congregation commits $250 a month to the direct aid ministry, and you want to help ten families, then each household could receive $25.

One other suggestion: If you decide to help financially, for example, with $75 for a power bill, pay the last $75 of the bill. Suppose the bill totaled $125. Ask the recipient to let you know when he/she has paid $50 ($125- $75 = $50) to the power company, and then send your check for $75. Why? If the remaining $50 of the bill is not paid, the power company will probably disconnect the power because the bill was not paid in full. You will have paid $75, and the family will still be without power. Check with the power companies in your area to determine exactly their policy if you decide to help families financially.

A former manager at United Ministries asked me to give her clear definitions for her program that helped with financial assistance and food. She said, "Once you give me the clear boundaries of the box in which I work, I'll have lots of freedom to move within that box." Working through these issues for clearly defining the box for successful service ministry will enhance the ministry for everyone involved, both giver and recipient.

Now that you have planned whom, how, and when to serve, it is time to begin implementing your direct aid ministry.

Implementing the Plan

You may have made wonderful plans. Many people are enthusiastic about the process to this point. Until you take the plunge and try out your ideas, you have only good intentions. You will develop a direct aid ministry only by doing it … after you have made thoughtful plans and created wise processes.

1. Whose permission do you need?

You've worked out whom, how, and when you want to provide direct aid. You have all your processes, procedures, and paperwork designed and ready to go. Now, whose permission do you need in order to begin the direct aid ministry?

Some faith groups encourage their membership to freely explore their individual calls to ministry and proceed with little or no permission or oversight. At the other end of the spectrum are congregations which require committee approval prior to the entire leadership group's consideration and vote. Some congregations have manuals of operations or constitutions which guide the entire decision-making process for everything. Others understand that when a plan has energy and commitment, those involved are encouraged to proceed without a second consideration. Only you can find out how your congregation works and who needs to see your fully developed proposal.

2. If you are working with a committee, how will the committee organize itself?

Once you have approval, implementation begins. Deciding how the committee or ministry team will function is key to its success. Actually assigning people to specific tasks or responsibilities will assure that everyone knows who is doing what. When members *assume* that somebody else is taking care of things, then, in actuality, nothing may be accomplished.

> Will the program have paid staff exclusively?
> Will paid staff be involved at all?
> Will the planning committee for the direct aid
> ministry divide itself into responsibility groups?
> If you are using volunteers, how will they be recruited
> and supervised?
> Who will provide the training?
> Who is responsible for scheduling them?
> Is fund raising to be part of this direct aid ministry?
> If so, how will you organize for that?
> How will you let the community know that this
> direct aid ministry is now available for them?
> Do you plan to interface with the existing human
> services community? If so, who will do that and
> when?

Warning!!!

All these plans will help you as you begin your direct aid ministry. However, things will happen that you did not anticipate and for which you do not have a ready solution. That's part of the faith, the fun, and the frustration.

One way to minimize some of these unexpected events is to begin small and grow into a larger direct aid ministry. Calling your initial effort a "pilot program" that will be evaluated after six or nine months will minimize some of the pressure for immediate success. With a pilot program, you are testing and learning and revising as needed. Pilot programs also give you a ready exit strategy if the process did not unfold as you had hoped and intended.

Summing Up

After you explored the "itch" and decided that direct service ministry is calling you and your congregation, you designed a well-thought-out process for loving your neighbor in very specific ways. You implemented a workable ministry within your congregation. Your reward for all this effort is seeing the faces of the people you help. You will receive an occasional "thanks." Even when you are unable to accommodate people's requests, treating them compassionately and kindly can be a wonderful gift both to them and to you.

Worksheet
Setting Up a Direct Aid Ministry

Exploring the "itch"

1. Why do you want to do this?
2. Are there other groups in your area doing similar things?
3. Is there a need for services in your area?
4. Are there enough people interested in this project to plan and carry it out?
5. Who else wants to do this?
6. Is there another organization with which you could partner?
7. Do you have support from the church leadership to explore this kind of ministry?

Whom/How/When to serve

1. Who is your target group?
2. What services do you want to provide?
3. How often may a household receive services?
4. What is your intake process?
5. When will you offer services?
6. How will you assist paying a bill, if you decide to help that way?
7. What is your budget?

Implementing the plan

1. Whose permission do you need?
2. If you are working with a committee, how will the committee organize itself?

Chapter Ten
Helping a Family in Need

*A*S A WAY TO live into Christ's challenge to love our neighbors, congregational groups might decide to look for ways to be involved with specific families or individuals who are living in poverty or who have significant problems.

Some congregations already work with individual families through a variety of ways: by adopting families at Christmas, by connecting with families in a nearby school, or by building a home for a family. Some of these partner relationships are successful for both the family and the group. Others can be frustrating.

Below is a process to help facilitate positive relationships between you—caring groups who want to help—and families or individuals who can use your help. Included are questions for you to work through *before* you meet your family. The answers are not as important as the *process* of answering the questions to the satisfaction of everyone involved. If you enter this ministry of compassion aware of what you hope will happen, the relationship has a better chance of being rich in rewards. If you enter with only a vague sense of "doing good," the possibilities are greater that frustrations will sabotage positive potential.

You can stand on holy ground with a needy family as you partner with them and with God.

Getting Started

When you decide to work with a family to help them improve their situation, it is tempting to meet the family and learn as you go. I have seen caring people, full of good intentions, begin an intense relationship only to become highly disenchanted and even angry with the family. Planning before meeting a family will improve the possibility for positive outcomes.

Note: A worksheet of the questions is at the end of this chapter.

1. How will the congregation find a family to work with?

Congregations may commit to working with a family who could use some help and then wonder how to find such a family. They know no one who is in financial need, or they never see needy people because of where the congregation's members live, work, and play. Other congregations will know many such families because of their own membership or geographic location.

Families who might benefit from help usually are connected in some way with one or more of the following: school social workers, child care providers, area social agencies, the United Way, or congregations in poorer areas in your community. If you contact one of these sources for information, you may discover they know a family intimately who might be interested in partnering with you to improve their situation. On the other hand, the organization's staff may have only a name or minimal knowledge of a family. In your discussions about this adventure of reaching out, think about the referral source in which you have the most confidence.

2. How will the congregation search for available resources?

Is someone in the congregation already connected with the helping agencies in the community? Does a member work in a charitable organization? Are there any social workers, counselors, or teachers who already know about the networks and services available in your community?

If there are no resources within your congregation, call an organization in the community, and ask for an appointment to talk with a staff member about the congregation's intention to work with a family. Ask for suggestions of possible resources. Better yet, develop an agreement that a member of the congregation's ministry team (who will be working with the family) can call the professional for help with next steps or other referral possibilities.

3. What community resources are available?

Your community may have a resource guide available that lists helping agencies and categories of assistance offered. Some United Way chapters produce such aids. Libraries, too, have accumulated information about community organizations. There may be a Web resource directory, or your community may have 2-1-1 access. Members of your congregation will often have information about services to meet certain needs because a friend or family member used those services.

4. Is there a human services agency professional who is willing to be a resource for the congregational group?

When you are able to work with a professional from a helping agency such as a cooperative ministry, Department of Social Services, or school social worker, you will have access to information that can be beneficial when working with a needy family. Through helping agencies, you can learn what is offered in the community, the requirements for acceptance into certain programs, and insights into some of the problems the family may be struggling with. This professional may be a member of your congregation or may be someone with whom your ministry team develops an intentional connection.

5. What is the congregation's financial commitment to a family? What are the limits?

This question requires significant conversation within the ministry team. Without setting limits prior to becoming involved with a family, your group can fracture over disagreements about what should and should not be done. For example, a strong ministry team will probably have someone with a huge heart who wants to reach out to help everyone. He or she will likely make decisions based on feelings and emotions, which can be powerful when walking on a painful journey with someone. A strong ministry team will probably have someone whose head rules what is done, when it is done, and how it is done. He or she is likely to make decisions based on information and evident facts. *Both* people are important on the ministry team. They *both* offer valuable insights and wisdom. If either takes over, the ministry team will not be as strong as when both are in balance.

Therefore, decisions about money need to be made before a real-life family is in the picture. For example, the ministry team might decide that the congregation will spend a maximum of one thousand dollars on the family, for whatever needs appear. Another group might decide that they will have $250 a month for six months available for the family. Another ministry team might decide that they will spend no money but provide personal support and relationship. They might assist with car rides for appointments, provide meals once or twice a month, or provide child care through the child development center.

There are no right or wrong decisions about financial assistance limits. The entire ministry team simply needs to agree on the decisions.

6. How will funds be accessed? Who can access them?

Once the ministry team knows what finances are available, clarify who can request and spend the funds. Can anyone on the team ask for a check to help the family? What if one person visits the family and discovers a need for prescription medication and uses some of the funds to purchase them? Another learns that one of the children needs field trip money and requests money. Another takes the mother grocery shopping. Before long, the entire amount available has been spent by the individual team members when the ministry team as a whole really preferred to pay the power bill.

Will ministry team members work from a reimbursement method? For example, a member takes the mother grocery shopping, pays for the groceries with a personal check, and then submits the receipt to the financial officer for reimbursement. Or will all payments be issued directly from the congregation's office or from the ministry team's treasurer?

Once again, there are no right or wrong decisions about this process. You simply need to decide before confusion or conflict develops about how money shall be spent.

7. Is there a length of time for the relationship commitment between the congregation and the family?

A relationship with a caring ministry team of a congregation may very well be the best thing that ever happened to a family in need. The family members may thrive under your care and attention. They may praise you over and over for what you are doing for them. On the other hand, they might begin acting as if you "owe" them your care and concern. One never knows how a family will react over time: with gratitude, a sense of entitlement, pleasure, guilt, or anger.

Knowing how long the ministry team intends to work with a family from the very beginning of the relationship is healthy for the family and the ministry team. The relationship might be six months. It might be a year. It might be until the mother completes her education. The limits need to be clearly established. Without limits, the ministry team might end the relationship too early out of frustration with the family and its behavior. Without limits, the relationship could last too long so that the family actually becomes dependent on the congregation and maybe even begins to manipulate the situation.

Of course, the limit can always be renegotiated—if the situation clearly warrants an extension. Even the new extension needs to be clearly defined.

One other reason to set time limits is that a ministry team that thrives in this kind of service to God will be able to work with more families as they complete their connection with one family and send them on in an improved condition. Another family will now be eligible to benefit from the care and compassion offered through your congregation and its ministry team.

8. Who is the primary contact for the working relationship within the congregation?

Even though every member of the ministry team might yearn to have a significant relationship with the family, the family can feel overwhelmed with too many people involved in their personal lives.

It may be hard enough to open up to one or two people. An entire committee might make the family feel as if they have been invaded... emotionally, physically, and spiritually. Especially at the beginning of the relationship-building process, only one or two people need to be the lead contacts from the ministry team with the family.

9. What is the congregation's expectation for the family's religious growth or congregational involvement?

Do you expect the family to attend your worship services and become a part of your congregation? Do you expect the family to attend a congregation of their choice while you are working with them? Is it okay for the family not to be involved in any kind of religious activity at all? Must the family be Christian? Will you invite the family to your congregation's programs without pressure for their attendance?

Each ministry team needs to clarify their expectations prior to working with a family. Unspoken or unacknowledged expectations can sabotage a healthy relationship between the family and the congregation.

10. Are there clear guidelines for congregational dos and don'ts for helping the family?

Some members in the congregation will be thrilled that their church is reaching out to families in need. They may offer a variety of help to the ministry team. Welcome their assistance with deep gratitude. Other members might decide to reach out to the family on their own without working through the ministry team. Though their intentions are good, they may actually negate some of the goals and focus between the ministry team and the family.

Some members of the family may tell their story to individuals within the congregation so that church members choose to give money directly to the family. The ministry team should strongly discourage congregational members from giving money directly to the family. Yet asking the congregation to refrain from reaching into their wallets for the family can be extremely difficult.

Members may say, "I have money. They don't. There is a need. I want to give. Isn't that what Jesus wants us to do?" The ministry team's response to and training for the congregation needs to affirm the congregation's desire to be involved. The congregation can be reminded that all assistance is to be coordinated with the ministry team. You can further explain that the ministry team knows more about the family's situation for making decisions about the most appropriate ways to help. Members who wish to contribute are encouraged to give to the ministry team's fund which is used when working with families. The congregation might even want to name the fund after a "Saint" in the history of the congregation.

You have thought through your process for helping a family. You have discussed your intentions for this kind of ministry. Everyone who will be directly involved clearly understands how you will work. Your plans are in writing, just in case misunderstandings arise later. Now you are ready to meet your family.

Developing a Relationship

Having the opportunity to build a relationship with a family who needs your help can be wonderfully enriching for everyone. Being aware of the family's need for autonomy and confidentiality is important. Loving with wisdom and compassion can go a long way for the relationship to be rewarding for everyone. By discussing the background explanations of these next questions prior to meeting your family, you will lay groundwork for a positive and healthy relationship with them.

1. What is the family's history? What is the family's story?

When you meet your family, introduce yourself, and share a bit about what motivated the congregation to become involved in this kind of caring ministry. Do not spend much time on introducing yourselves because this is just the beginning of building a relationship with your family. As time develops, you will each learn more about the other.

Ask your family to tell you about themselves. Listen empathetically. Acknowledge that you are hearing their feelings as they tell their story. You will not hear the entire story on this visit. As the relationship develops, you will learn more about the situations underlying the parts of the story you hear today. For now, accept the story exactly as they tell it. You might ask questions for clarification, but generally this is not the time to ask, "Why?" You are letting the family guide the flow of this first meeting.

Do not take notes at this meeting except for the kinds of things that require correct information: names of family members, birth dates, level of education, etc. Taking extensive notes may make the family uneasy since they won't know what you're writing.

One other thing: You will need to earn trust from your family. They may have misgivings about anyone reaching into their family situation. They may fear that you will learn something that will result in their children being taken away from them. They may have experienced situations of abuse or neglect so that they are highly suspicious of authority figures. They may have known people who made promises to them and then did not keep those promises. Only through consistent, caring, *and* honest relationship building will the family begin to trust you so that true ministry can begin. Only through trusting relationships can opportunities for new life take root.

2. Is there an existing format for obtaining basic information (Social Security numbers, income, birth dates, etc.)?

If you connected with the family through an agency or social worker, you may already have basic facts through the referral source. If confidentiality laws protect the information at the agency, ask for their standard intake form, which you can fill out as you gather data on the family.

3. What are the family's dreams for themselves? Are the dreams realistic?

When you first ask this question of the family, you may get only a blank stare from them. People who have been concerned about basic survival may have no dreams. They may be able to concentrate only on getting through the day. Their primary concerns might be: "Do I have enough food for my family *today*?" "Do we have a roof over our heads?" "Can I get my child to health care *today*?" "Will I get beat up *today*?"

Some of the dreams may seem very unrealistic to you. I was working with some women who were prostitutes and/or addicts. I asked them to share their dreams with me. At first, I saw only blank faces. Then one woman ventured to share her dream. She described a cottage with a white picket fence. Several others said they wanted to work in an office. One woman was testing me when she said that her dream was to be a madam and own her own house of prostitution! (I did not know her real name for six months, only her street name.)

I was honestly puzzled why someone who was an addict or a prostitute would have as her life dream to work in an office. I knew that entry-level office positions did not pay well. On further research, I learned that dreams for office work grew out of the knowledge that people who work in offices dress nicely, have job titles, work in air-conditioning, usually sit rather than stand, and often have regular work hours. The women perceived that people who work in an office are smart and have power and authority. After all, when you need medical care, you go to the doctor's *office*; when you need legal assistance, you go to the lawyer's *office*; or if you need food stamps, you go to the food stamp *office*.

Learning the family's dreams can help you discern what may be important to them. You can use the dream to help them understand what next steps are possible for realizing their goals. For example, if the family's dream is home ownership, you can review their income level and discuss what must happen to increase their earning potential (education? job training? building a good work history?). You can look at their credit report and work with them on repairing bad credit, if needed, which could lead to conversations about budgeting, smart shopping, avoiding predatory lenders, etc. A trusting relationship must first exist before any of these goals can be claimed. Nevertheless, the dream can help develop a flowchart for planning and next steps.

4. What are the congregation's dreams for the family? Are the dreams realistic?

Does the congregation envision turning this family into a strong middle-class family with middle-class values? That likely will not happen. Does the congregation envision helping the family reach their own self-determined goals, even if the goals might be different from those the congregation could fully embrace? Without knowing the congregation's goals, the ministry team will have difficulty evaluating the success of the ministry with the family. False assumptions may derail the entire relationship.

5. *What are the strengths in the family? How will they be used to accomplish success?*

Every family has resources and strengths. They may be highly spiritual. They may be emotionally strong. Their health might be very good. They may truly love, respect, and care about each other. One person might be the stabilizing force within the family. Another family member might be adept at bringing laughter and joy into their circle. Focus on the strengths rather than the weaknesses within the family. Use their strengths to help the family and the ministry team accomplish the tasks and goals agreed upon.

6. *Who will orient the family regarding the working relationship process?*

Someone from the ministry team needs to be designated as the spokesperson for the group in order to give a single consistent message to the family. That representative might ask for assistance from an agency professional, especially if that staff person already has a working relationship with the family. The family and the ministry team need to have a clear understanding of the limits and intentions of the partnership process. As long as everyone understands the partnership for creating new opportunities, the bumps along the way should not be as rough as they could be when unrealistic expectations and assumptions have not been addressed.

7. *Are lines of contact and communication between congregation members and the family clearly defined and established?*

Who may the family contact and how should that contact be made? Which committee member's phone number will be given to the family? Are there certain times of day or days of the week that are more appropriate for contact than others? Does the family know specific times of day or the week when contact is not welcome? Can a family member who is working receive phone messages at work?

What will happen within the ministry team if the family begins calling individual team members or even members of the congregation? How will the team handle this with the family?

8. What are the roles of the various members of the ministry team in working with this family?

One member of the ministry team might be the treasurer for the group. Another might like to transport the family when necessary. Still another may be adept at teaching homemaking and cooking skills. Someone might be a great advocate in terms of overcoming bureaucratic hurdles. Another member might be the ideal person for communicating with the congregation as a whole, in a positive and not paternalistic way. Assess the strengths and skills within the ministry team, and use those to the fullest.

9. How will confidentiality be addressed and maintained?

Occasionally a ministry team of a congregation will begin working with a family and believe that all the details of the family's situation should be shared with the entire church. The assumption is that every member wants and needs to know what is happening in the name of the church. This information may be given in great detail, or it may be released inadvertently in subtle ways such as including specific petitions for the family during the pastoral prayer in worship. Other team members might share a funny happening or something they found profoundly moving, thereby violating the trust of the family. Unbeknownst to the ministry team, the family may be offended by being the subject of such conversation.

Generally only people who *need* to know are the ones who receive important information. When in doubt about sharing details of the family's life beyond the ministry team—don't. Admonish team members to refrain from sharing too much information even with their own families. The family receiving assistance has human dignity and pride. The ministry team needs to protect the family's privacy to the greatest extent possible.

Carefully and thoughtfully building a caring relationship with your family will allay feelings of anger and mistrust when things don't go as planned. When people know you care, they will work with you for the good of their family in a remarkable way. When people believe that you truly want what's best for them, they will forgive your honest missteps in your efforts to befriend and nurture them.

Note: The Cathy Exercise at the end of this chapter will give you a hint of issues and problems you might confront when working with a family.

Maintaining a Healthy Process

Occasionally a relationship with a family can begin to develop negative dynamics within it. At United Ministries we linked a caring volunteer with an elderly couple who needed some help. As the relationship developed, it became clear that the couple was doing fine and no longer needed the volunteer's assistance. In fact, they began to dread his visits. The staff member realized the volunteer was beginning to meet his own needs for connection and being indispensable at the expense of the couple. The volunteer became highly resistant when told he was no longer to visit the couple. The time for the relationship was over. An unhealthy relationship could no longer continue.

A healthy relationship is good for all!

1. What is the overall goal agreed upon between the congregation and the family?

Provided the ministry team and the family have built a trusting relationship and developed clarity about each person's responsibility in the family and in the ministry team, put the plan with goals and expectations in *writing*. There is an old adage that if something was not in writing, it did not happen. Make sure that everyone has copies of the "formal" document.

2. Is there a process for helping the family move from high dependency to no dependency?

Hopefully as the ministry team was beginning to plan for working with a family, you considered a couple of the mantras listed in Chapter 7: "Do not do something for the family which the family can and should do for itself" and "Poor planning on your part does not constitute an emergency on mine." You talked about the dangers of the family using you as an open bank. The team accepted the serious task of helping the family learn to take advantage of the life-changing opportunities offered to them.

Occasionally the ministry team might find it helpful to have a human services professional help debrief your experiences. Talking about your family with someone who is both professional and passionate about helping families in need can be eye-opening. With more objectivity, the professional can point out ways the ministry team is inadvertently encouraging dependency, despite good intentions for helping the family. We all can develop blind spots when we are in a relationship with others.

Stay focused on the agreed goals and time limits.

3. Who will conduct debriefing sessions with the congregation?

The chairperson of the ministry team, the minister of the congregation, or a human services professional within the congregation may give updates as appropriate and needed. Some happenings may provide further educational or ministry opportunities within the congregation as members learn more about issues of poverty.

4. Who will conduct regular debriefing sessions with the family?

Either the team member who has primary contact with the family or a professional from a helping agency may be the most appropriate person to spend time processing the experience with the family. Another person in the congregation—but not on the ministry team—might be an obvious choice to hear the family's concerns and joys about the process.

Clarity about your task before you have a partner family will make you more comfortable about what you are doing. Common understanding will enhance your credibility with the family. They will more likely believe that you know what you are doing. Sticking to your agreed plans helps ensure positive outcomes. Being willing, when necessary, to adapt with thoughtful intentions is essential. Staying focused at all times on building and growing positive and healthy relationships with family members is the foundation of everything else you do with and for them. You will grow in unbelievable ways because of their relationship with you.

Possible Pitfalls

The old saying has it that even the best-laid plans often go astray. With that in mind, there are some pitfalls that can sabotage your best efforts.

1. The congregation has "all the answers" for solving the problems in another person's life.

No one in the congregation has had the exact same experiences as the family. They don't share the same background. With that as fact, how could anyone else know what is best for the family? Any solution which might work for the person with "all the answers" may be counterproductive for someone with totally different realities.

Once the ministry team has developed their clear guidelines, the congregation may benefit from having the process explained. The minister can reinforce the ministry team's intentions and processes through his or her teaching, preaching, and meetings. The message will need to be given frequently and by a variety of voices that the congregation's ministry team has clearly thought out whom, how, and when it will help. Set and maintain clear boundaries about the process with the congregation. Caring people who do not abide by the guidelines developed by the ministry team may in fact undermine the team's good work.

2. Individual congregation members may circumvent the process (by giving their own money directly to the family, for example).

When United Ministries began using volunteers to interview people who needed help with rent, utilities, prescriptions, heat, or food, the staff encountered an unexpected problem. Some volunteers wanted to give money from their pocket to the person they were interviewing. They were likely to do this when the person needed more than the usual allotment from United Ministries or if the person seeking assistance reminded the volunteer of his child, parent, or grandchild. When a volunteer talked with someone who seemed to have insurmountable problems, she was likely to pull out her checkbook.

We had to teach the volunteers that giving directly to program participants was not *fair*. We acknowledged that we did not treat everyone equally. Some received more assistance than others based on their personal situations. However, we wanted to treat everyone fairly. The program participant who was lucky enough to be interviewed by someone with income adequate to give directly got more assistance. The person whose interviewer did not reach into his or her pocket was not so lucky. It simply was not fair. We encouraged volunteers with abundant resources to give directly to the program. We underscored that if the program had all the resources it needed, then we could substantially increase our help to everyone!

3. The problems which first present themselves may not be the fundamental problems.

Family members might be embarrassed to tell the ministry team what is really going on. They may fear that if the ministry team knew other issues within the household, the team might refuse to work with them. Because the overruling value for people in long-term poverty is relationship, the family at first may tell only what they believe the ministry team wants to hear. They want to be liked. They believe that they will be helped if the team has positive feelings about them.

4. The congregation may discover issues or activities with which they are extremely uncomfortable.

The team may have to decide whether to continue working with a family if they discover illegal activity, drug abuse, or physical abuse. Each team will need to assess its willingness and capacity to deal with difficult situations.

5. The family may resent having someone "tell them what to do."

Building a strong relationship with the family greatly improves the willingness of the family to listen. The ministry team also needs to listen intently and empathetically to the family in order to hear both what is being said and what is being implied or avoided. An approach which models friendship or coaching may be more helpful than an authoritarian style.

No one can change anyone else. The ministry team can offer opportunities to change. The decision on whether to work toward change rests with the family.

6. *The family may try to prolong the relationship beyond the agreed time.*

Being very clear from the outset about the length of the formal relationship is essential. Standing firm to that commitment increases the chances that the family will keep working on its situation because they know that their time is ending soon. If there are *extremely* valid reasons to add to or renegotiate the length of the commitment, the renewal requires definite and specific new ending dates. Using ambiguous endings such as when Mom finishes school or when Dad gets a job allow for undefined extensions. Mom may not finish school for years, or Dad's job may be part-time and temporary. The more clearly the ending is defined, the easier it is to adhere to the decision.

7. *Taking on more than you can handle.*

As the relationship develops and more and more issues become evident, the ministry team may realize that it is not equipped to deal with the magnitude of the problems. At this point, conversations with helping agency professionals will be essential in deciding how or whether the ministry team can continue to work with the family.

Deciding to help a family in deep and life-enhancing ways is rewarding, challenging, frustrating, and ultimately life-giving. The more clarity you have about the entire process, the more fulfilling your work with a family will be. You and your congregation will be enriched through the opportunity to reach out in ways that Jesus would commend.

Worksheet
Helping a Family in Need

Getting Started

1. How will the congregation find a family to work with?
2. How will the congregation search for available resources?
3. What community resources are available?
4. Is there a human services agency professional who is willing to be a resource for the congregational group?
5. What is the congregation's financial commitment to a family? What are the limits?
6. How will funds be accessed? Who can access them?
7. Is there a length of time for the relationship commitment between the congregation and the family?
8. Who is/are the primary contact(s) for the working relationship within the congregation?
9. What is the congregation's expectation for the family's religious growth or congregational involvement?
10. Are there clear guidelines for congregational dos and don'ts for helping the family?

Developing a Relationship

1. What is the family history? What is the family's story?
2. Is there an existing format for obtaining basic information (social security numbers, income, birth dates, etc.)?

3. What are the family's dreams for themselves? Are the dreams realistic?
4. What are the congregation's dreams for the family? Are the dreams realistic?
5. What are the strengths in the family? How will they be used to accomplish success?
6. Who will orient the family regarding the working relationship process?
7. Are lines of contact and communication between congregation members and the family clearly defined and established?
8. What are the roles of the various members of the congregation in working with this family?
9. How will confidentiality be addressed and maintained?

Maintaining a Healthy Process

1. What is the overall goal agreed upon between the congregation and the family?
2. Is there a process for helping the family move from high dependency to no dependency?
3. Who will conduct debriefing sessions with the congregation?
4. Who will conduct regular debriefing sessions with the family?

Exercise

Cathy

This exercise is helpful in realizing that the downward spiral of poverty is difficult to overcome. There rarely is just *one thing* to be done to alter a situation for the good. Getting through "the system" often requires assistance that may not be readily available. A person in need may not know where or how to access services, such as case management, even when they are offered in the community. People who have never faced the challenges of poverty may not realize the intensity of those challenges or the seemingly insurmountable barriers to overcoming the challenges.

Cathy is a young woman who needs your help. You must decide how best to help her overcome the obstacles in her life. By helping her, you'll glimpse how difficult living in poverty can be.

Instructions: Read the description of Cathy. Put the tasks for her in order of priority, so she can improve her life.

Cathy
is 26 years old and is four months pregnant. She was living with her boyfriend in a small trailer until the boyfriend beat her up and threw her out. The boyfriend became angry when he found out that Cathy was pregnant, and he suspected he was not the father of the child. Cathy spent the next three nights staying with various friends. Then she stayed in several motels until her money ran out.

She is now staying with a cousin who lives in government housing with her family of six. Cathy sleeps on a couch and is afraid that the housing manager will find out about her and will evict the entire family. Cathy's mother is dead, and she doesn't know where her father is.

Cathy has two other children who have been placed in foster care. The younger child tested positive for drugs at birth, so Cathy is currently on probation for giving birth to a "crack baby." Although Cathy has been clean for the past two months, she is in violation of her probation because she has not been to her drug treatment class for the past month.

Cathy has never held a job for more than a few months and has no marketable skills, but she does have a high school diploma. She has never had a driver's license, and her boyfriend flushed the contents of her wallet down the toilet when he threw her out. Cathy has been emotionally and sexually abused her entire life. She has a very low opinion of herself. She lacks self-confidence and sees no way out of her trouble.

What will you do to help Cathy?

Prioritize the following list of items that Cathy may need to move toward self sufficiency. (Number 1 is the most important, and number 19 is the least important.)

Counseling
Medical Care
Clothing
Spiritual Guidance
Furniture
Child Care
Transportation
Addiction Aftercare
Mailing Address
Job Training

Employment
Temporary Shelter
Legal Aid
Addiction Treatment
ID papers
Permanent Housing
Utility Deposits
Rent Deposits
Food Stamps

Reflection

After you have wrestled with the process, consider your priorities. Why did you choose the first three things on your list?

Below is a suggested priority list which is based on the three interconnecting tasks of survival, stabilization, and barrier removal.

Survival: A person must remain alive in order to be helped.

Stabilization: If the situation is not stable, then accessing life-changing opportunities and success is difficult, if not impossible.

Barrier Removal: If someone lacks transportation, funds for tuition, money management skills, health care, or child care, he or she must have help to overcome these barriers in order to have significant, substantive change in his or her life.

Priorities for Cathy

There is no right sequence for Cathy. However, certain issues must be addressed in clusters. The tasks may not come together in the suggested order because of timing issues, regulations such as a needed document that is not yet accessible, or availability of appointments.

Basic Survival

Temporary Shelter (night shelters, battered women's shelters, etc.)
Medical Care (free medical clinics, community health centers, obstetrics clinics associated with hospitals, etc.)
Clothing (thrift stores, clothes closets, garage sales, etc.)

Stabilization

Transportation (public transportation, car rides by volunteers, etc)
Food Stamps (through departments of social/human services)
Mailing address (through shelters for people who are homeless or by general delivery at post offices)
Identification papers (highway departments for picture ID, social security cards through Social Security Administration, birth certificates; locations vary by state)

Job training (human service training programs,
technical/community colleges, Goodwill, etc.)
Employment (state employment offices, human service
organizations with job assistance programs, etc.)
Permanent housing (Hopefully a job will enable
Cathy to pay cheap rent, or maybe she can double up
with someone.)
Rent deposits (cooperative ministries, denominational
charities, human service agencies, etc.)
Utility deposits (cooperative ministries, denominational
charities, human service agencies, etc.)
Furniture (thrift stores, garage sales, etc.)
Addiction aftercare ... to help prevent a relapse
(Alcoholics Anonymous, Narcotics Anonymous,
treatment programs offered in the area, etc.)

Barrier Removal

Legal Aid (to help regain custody of her children)
Temporary Aid to Needy Families (TANF) (Upon
the birth of her child, Cathy may qualify for TANF
assistance and for subsidized housing.)
Counseling (mental health centers, family counseling
centers, etc.)
Spiritual Guidance (through Cathy's own
congregation or the volunteers and staff at faith-based
organizations)
Child care (state-offered vouchers, congregational-
based child-care centers, human service centers, etc.)
Addiction Treatment ... if Cathy relapses (provided
by treatment centers, Alcoholics Anonymous, and/or
area inpatient treatment hospitals, etc.)

Exercise Questions to Consider

1. What would have helped Cathy handle all these tasks?

2. Does your community have all the resources that Cathy needs?

3. What was most difficult about this exercise for you?

4. How would the process you developed help a person like Cathy?

Chapter Eleven
Evaluating Benevolence Requests

YOU AND YOUR CONGREGATION likely receive requests for financial support from many different groups and individuals. The leadership in congregations or the pastor is charged with deciding who, when, and how to help. How will you decide where to direct your benevolences? Who will receive your charitable gifts?

One day I was walking across a parking lot, and a car pulled alongside me. The driver was a minister friend of mine. He rolled down the window, leaned out the window on his arm, and said, "Beth, my church is getting bombarded with requests from all kinds of agencies who are requesting money. I really believe in your organization and want to continue to support it. However, I need some help for my leadership team in making decisions about how we give our benevolence dollars. Can you help?"

At the time of the request, I had a seminary intern, Carolyn Mathis, working with me. She and I developed a series of questions that are presented here in this chapter. A number of congregations and benevolence committees have used them as a beginning point for their decision-making process.

Note: A worksheet of the questions is at the end of this chapter.

Background of Your Congregation

It's important to know your faith community when deciding which organizations you will support with the congregation's charitable dollars.

1. What is the mission of your congregation?

The mission of your congregation is not necessarily what the printed statement in official documents says. The mission statement which most Christian churches state in one way or another is: "We are the body of Christ who is our head. We will worship, learn, pray, serve, and fellowship together in order to grow in faith and service to our Lord."

As important as all those beliefs and words are, they do not really talk about the distinct mission of your individual worshiping community. Your mission is the focus of your congregation at *this* time and in *this* place. Some ways your faith group may define its mission are:

> To have a strong, energetic ministry with older adults.
> To minister primarily to families through terrific
> programs for children and youth.
> To bring people to faith in Jesus Christ.
> To engage in active social justice ministries.

There are other reasons why groups of people come together and continue to stay together as a body of faith. What is your mission?

2. How does this project fit into your overall mission?

When you are clear about what your particular mission is, you may discover some organizations that request financial support do not align with who you are. For example, a congregation whose mission is saving souls may choose not to give resources to an organization using little or no religious vocabulary in its work or its publicity. On the other hand, a congregation that values inclusivity might enjoy partnership with a program working with women who struggle to overcome addiction and prostitution.

Your understanding of mission is the main measuring tool for evaluating requests for benevolences. The groups to whom you give resources should be understood as extensions of your congregation's mission in the community and the world.

Source of the Request

Requests for funds come in many forms and from many sources. You may receive an appeal letter signed by someone you've never heard of. You may receive a personal visit from a representative of a group seeking funding. After hearing an impassioned speech about a significant ministry, a member may request that your church support the work. A group of members may want to establish a new helping ministry and seek church financial support.

Sometimes members of the congregation will decide to give based on who is asking. We know that when certain people ask, a congregation is more likely to fund the pet program, organization, or ministry—even if the request does not fit the mission of the church.

1. Who is asking you to consider this cause, group, or agency? Some of the questions to discuss include:

Does this request come from an active group in the church?
Is the request simply a generic form letter received from an organization?
Is there any validity in the source of the request?
Does the source of the request suggest why this cause should or should not be considered?

2. Would you consider the request if someone else was asking?

Many congregations put things into budgets because the right person at the right time pushed for them to be included. If Mrs. I. M. Power wants a program or a mission opportunity to receive financial support from the congregation, her project will be included. Whenever Tim Wimp makes a request for a program, his concerns are usually overlooked. Benevolence items may remain in a budget for years because someone in the past included them. The support was never questioned again or evaluated for continuation.

3. What personal concerns does this organization address?

If your congregation has a significant number of teens in it, for example, the congregation might choose to get involved with a teenage pregnancy prevention program. Congregations whose members have friends or family struggling to live with drug dependencies might support an organization concerned with addiction treatment and follow-up.

Looking at a request based on the merits of the request rather than on personality is essential for making wise and compassionate decisions about giving your benevolences.

Involvement of Your Congregation

Congregations may choose to give money. Increasing numbers of church leaders and lay members, however, want to do more than give money. They want personal involvement. They seek to support agencies and programs that can engage members of their congregation.

1. What call(s) to ministry does this organization address?

Each faith body will have understandings of how best to serve God and nurture those things most sacred in its life. Calls to ministry within the congregation might include growing spiritually, serving God through service to others, helping the church claim its life as a body of faith, and/or teaching and growing disciples. Some of the questions you may consider are:

> Does the organization which is requesting financial support address any of our calls to ministry?
> Does the organization offer opportunities for volunteers to get involved in direct service with people in need?
> Does it offer opportunities to grow spiritually?
> Does it offer venues for evangelism?

2. *What opportunities for personal involvement of members of your congregation does this project offer? Some of your considerations might be:*

> How can your members get involved?
> Hands-on service?
> Policy making?
> Letter writing?
> Group discussions?
> Collecting needed items?
> Providing space?
> Prayer?
> Other?

When a congregation is able to yoke its financial support with its understanding of its mission within the community and the world, it claims a partnership in a broader kind of ministry than it is able to do alone. By offering its members challenges through active involvement in the organizations and programs it financially supports, a church provides its members a way to explore their own God-given calls to service. A congregation undergirds its sense of stewardship and service by connecting members' gifts of time, talents, and treasure to its mission within its walls and beyond.

Organizational Information

An organization may align well with the church's understanding of its mission in the world. It may offer opportunities for members to be involved in active, hands-on service. However, it may not have the internal structure for doing what it says it does. The organization may not be effective or efficient. It may not instill confidence within donors, volunteers, or program participants because of its lack of quality management.

Is this organization managed well? This question is primary. As good stewards of money given for holy work, people who are charged with making decisions about spending money obviously want to know that the money is being used well on important things. Conscientious congregations look intentionally at the organizations and programs they align with through money and support. Some of the ways you can study an organization are:

> Request a copy of the organization's annual report including service figures.
> Ask to see the latest prepared audit.
> Seek personal testimony about the organization from people you know.
> Seek the opinions of members who volunteer in the organization. They see the internal workings of an organization.
> Arrange an on-site visit.
> Talk with staff, with volunteers, and with program participants. Listen to what you hear, and pay attention to what you see.
> What kinds of feelings do you have after your visit? Positive? Negative? Questioning?

Organizations and programs that are reputable and well managed welcome review by congregations and other donors. They are open with information. When an agency or service ministry is reticent about providing requested information, you may consider that to be a warning flag worth pursuing. You certainly want your questions answered so that you can report to the decision-making body with full confidence.

Possible Results of Deciding to Support a Request

Choosing to invest in another organization or service ministry involves more than putting a dollar amount in the budget. It can involve risks. It can also offer huge benefits. For example, giving financial support to certain projects or programs may draw attention to the congregation within the community in amazing and powerful ways. It can expand or diminish a congregation's ministry in the community.

1. *If you decide to contribute to this project, will you give a one-time special offering or put the project in the annual budget?*

The leadership in some congregations acknowledges that their members will actually give more money to an organization with a special offering or event rather than if the request is included in the budget. Sometimes a church will decide to support a program for a limited time. For example, the members may decide to provide funds for the start-up phase of a program with the understanding that after two years their commitment is over.

2. *How and when will you evaluate (if you contribute)?*

Some of the questions you might consider are:

> How will you evaluate your involvement in this project?
> Will this be one other thing which gets included in the budget and remains there for decades?
> Will the number of congregation members involved in this opportunity be important?
> Will level of enthusiasm for the project among education classes, Bible study groups, or the leadership be a deciding factor?
> Are there opportunities for youth volunteer missions?
> Are there ways for senior members of the congregation to be engaged?
> What other criteria are important for a successful collaboration between the congregation and this organization?
> How will you evaluate the project itself on a continuing basis?
> Is the number of people served by the program essential for an ongoing partnership?
> Are the program outcomes worth looking at?
> What criteria will you use to evaluate this opportunity?

3. What kind of publicity will this project provide for your congregation?

    a. Positive: Will this project reflect well on your congregation?

    b. Negative: Will this project anger others when you choose to lend your support?

4. What are the risks?

One congregation decided to involve itself deeply with programs for people who struggled to live with various mental illnesses. To that end, members decided to support financially the purchase and renovation of apartments for people who were being supervised for long-term mental illnesses. The apartments would allow residents with mental health issues to function independently with social support.

The challenge for the congregation was that the apartments were in a neighborhood that did not want "those people" living in their midst. The neighborhood residents had political and media clout. Even so, the congregation put considerable monies toward the purchase of the apartments and allowed its name to be associated with the project. They considered they were following in Jesus' footsteps of casting out demons. They wanted people to live healthy lives. The risks involved were, for them, part of serving their Lord Jesus Christ.

Ultimately the apartments were converted for the new residents, who, as it turns out, are model neighbors. The church has since taken other bold and innovative steps in its ministry of trying to model the kingdom of God. They decided the risks were worth their trying to serve God.

Just because risks are involved is no reason not to support a worthy endeavor. Knowing what those risks are beforehand is prudent when deciding to link your name and support. You can discern whether there are ways to minimize those risks, or you can determine ways to address them head on.

5. What are the opportunities?

Questions you may consider are:

Does this program or organization expand your own mission as a faith body?

Will it give members ways to grow in their own faith?
Will it nurture new disciples?
Will it help people who are very comfortable in their
lives to be shaken into new ways of serving God?

One congregation added an apartment for homeless families to its facilities. The apartment provides a safe home as families transition from the streets (or living in their car) to a place of their own. The congregation enjoys the opportunity to interact with these folks in their midst who need their support. One member quipped, "The Bible says that we are to reach out to poor people. I didn't know any poor people, but now I do!"

We understand that where a congregation chooses to put some of its money can be very important to members and potential members. Some people choose a church because of the public witness it offers. Being known as a congregation that supports specific causes will be very important to certain folks. Offering opportunities to volunteer in the community as part of a member's faith journey is essential for others. Your benevolences can have positive impact on your life as a congregation.

Discussing the issues that underlie decisions about how to spend benevolences can be a faithful journey. Thinking about your congregation's mission, its desire to engage members in service ministry, and its perceived call from God for involvement in the community and in the world can enrich one's understanding of walking the way of Jesus. Getting involved with the organizations, programs, service ministries, and agencies that receive your financial support can open members' hearts and minds beyond the walls of the particular congregation. Using your benevolence dollars to serve God and your neighbors is a joyful occupation!

Worksheet
Evaluating Benevolence Requests

Background of Our Congregation

1. What is the mission of our congregation?

2. How does this project fit into our overall mission?

Source of the Request

1. Who is asking us to consider this cause, group, or agency?

2. Would we consider the request if someone else was asking?

3. What personal concerns does this organization address?

Involvement of Our Congregation

1. What call(s) to ministry does this organization address?

2. What opportunities for personal involvement of members of our congregation does this project offer?

Organizational Information

Is this organization managed well?
    Annual report
    Service figures
    Audit
    Personal testimony
    On-site visit

Possible Results of Deciding to Support a Request

    1. If we decide to contribute to this project, will we give a one time special offering, or shall we put it in the annual budget?

    2. How and when will we evaluate (if we contribute):
        Our involvement in this project?
        The project itself on a continuing basis?

    3. What kind of publicity will this project provide for our congregation?
        a. Positive
        b. Negative

    4. What are the risks?

    5. What are the opportunities?

Chapter Twelve
Motivating Members to Help

Y OU CAN HELP MEMBERS get involved in loving their neighbors in a variety of ways. Some are comparatively easy in terms of time commitment. They seem small in that they require minimal personal involvement. You can ask members to respond by collecting items, by attending a meeting to learn about community service, or by giving to a special offering. Other kinds of involvement require major time and commitment. People may volunteer regularly in a program or commit to planning a major new ministry emphasis for the church. Individuals who are highly motivated to love their neighbors are likely to reap high rewards in satisfaction and sense of accomplishment. They will get as much out of the significant relationships they develop as do the people they are serving.

How Groups Can Help

After people have been inspired by a speaker, a Bible study, a film, or a book to do something, then you can give them ideas about ways they can get more involved in loving their neighbor. Members can collectively decide to do one or more of the following:

1. Collect toiletries (soap, towels, shampoo, toothpaste, tooth brushes, etc.) for homeless people or homeless service providers.

2. Collect food items for food pantries or soup kitchens.
3. Promote and participate in fund-raising events hosted by organizations supported by your congregation.
4. Invite human services providers to speak, preach, teach, or lead a workshop.
5. Ask a helping agency to allow you to host your meeting on their premises. While there, tour the facilities.
6. Encourage congregation members to get involved through helping agencies' committees, direct services, fund-raiser events, pro bono services for their program participants, etc.
7. In addition to regular budgetary contributions from your congregation, develop "creative" ways to financially support helping agencies (bazaars, suppers, etc.).
8. Volunteer and recruit volunteers for positions from volunteer job listings at helping agencies.
9. Ask helping agencies for specific projects or needs in which your congregation members could participate.
10. Include special events of helping agencies in your congregation's calendar bulletin, newsletter, or Web site.
11. Other?

Sometimes getting a group involved in a special, one-time, limited project can open the doors to service which provides in-depth opportunities for building long-term relationships between your members and people who need your help.

How Individuals Can Help

An individual may want to be involved whether or not the group chooses to do something. The variety of options include:

1. *Take up collections of money, items needed by individuals or helping agencies, or letters.*

> Give stock or cash.
> "Pass the basket" at work, in your neighborhood, at your civic club, etc.
> Host a fundraiser (carnival, bake sale, talent show, etc.).
> Contact people who are passionate for your issue and who will make a gift.
> Collect books, school supplies, clothing, food items, toiletry items, or household goods.
> Provide gift cards or work gear.
> Advocate through an offering of letters for your issue or concern.

2. *Give your time.*

> Volunteer in an organization which is working in the area of your passion.
> Commit to a specific time-bound project.
> Serve on a committee, task force, or board of directors.
> Ignite others to your issue or concern in your workplace, neighborhood, civic groups, social groups, or congregation.
> Disseminate information to appropriate decision makers.
> Write letters to the editor.

3. *Meet and talk with people who are suffering.*

> Volunteer with an organization working with people you care about.
> Look for opportunities in your neighborhood, workplace, or place of worship to converse with someone who is hurting.
> Read stories, books, and articles about people who are suffering. Allow them into your heart.

4. Learn more about your issue of passion.

Talk with people who are already working in the area of your interest.

Listen carefully and deeply before making suggestions for solutions.

Look for the "underbelly" of whatever ideas you develop. Most good solutions also have negative impacts. Can you reduce the downside?

Research your issue so that you know what advocates for and advocates against think and believe.

Create forums where ideas can be shared and discussed.

5. Become aware of how your life impacts others.

Buy fairly traded products.

Consider the concept that cheap food, clothing, and other items for us means that workers are not paid adequate wages.

Offer someone a job, and work with him or her in learning how to keep it.

Use resources (material and environmental) in ways that benefit the greater good. For example, ask yourself when you buy, "Do I need it, or could that money help someone else?"

Reduce your energy consumption.

6. Provide prayer, spiritual, emotional, and social support for:

People on the "front lines" addressing the area of your passion.

Groups within your congregation who are involved in serving others.

Community leaders and politicians who work to make the changes you believe in.

When you help an individual find his or her own area of service to others, you are loving your neighbor. By offering members a variety of ways to get involved with neighbors who are poor, you are helping them grow into their God-given challenges. Watching people blossom as they connect with others who are often invisible is a real blessing!

When Members Do Not Help

Sometimes no matter what you do or offer as opportunities for service to others in your community, members just don't step up to the wonderful opportunities available. In the process of developing a service ministry, you, your congregation's leadership, or the mission ministry team may become dismayed that not everyone in the congregation is as enthused and committed as you are. You are challenged by trying to connect with members who lack interest. There are a variety of things to consider when trying to motivate members.

Note: "Why I Am Afraid to Get Involved" is an exercise at the end of this chapter.

Discover What "Church" Means to Members

Individual members align with a church for a variety of reasons. Their understanding of church comes, in part, from their reasons for joining the congregation. They seek fellowship or comfort. They want activities for their children. They yearn for a place where there are clear answers to life's problems. They want a place for their wedding or funeral. There are probably as many understandings within a local congregation of what church means as there are members. The official church documents might expound the truths which have come down through the ages, but that does not necessarily mean the members fully claim those.

Some members simply need the church to be there for them in times of crisis or celebration: death, illness, weddings, etc. They do not expect or want any other demands or interactions. Others do not realize they are expected to do anything other than show up at service a couple of times a month (or twice a year!) and give some money once in a while.

Other members see the church as a place of nurture for their spiritual lives which encourages deep faith. They are focused on the inward journeys of prayer, Bible study, meditation, etc. Some cloistered nuns once ventured into their immediate community to see where homeless people "lived," to see the poverty that was hidden from them, and to witness for themselves the hurting which was there. At the end of the tour, they asked for the names of all the staff who worked in the organization that had arranged the poverty tour for them. The religious sisters then committed to pray for each staff member by name every day for strength in their work.

Others see the purpose of the church as educating and growing the next generation of faithful people. Their intention is to instill a sense of the heritage, beliefs, and commitments of the church to everyone who comes in the door. They want to maintain and enhance the truth and beauty of religion. Service happens for them *within* the walls of the congregation rather than on the outside.

All kinds of people connect themselves to congregations for all kinds of reasons. Through offering a variety of ways to get involved with differing requirements of time, resources, and commitment, you develop ways to infuse commitment and enthusiasm for serving others within the membership. You trust God to nudge people in the way they need to be nudged and for the purposes God is waiting to reveal. You then engage those who are ready *now* to be involved.

Train the Untrained

Some members would like to be involved in serving others. They would like to help build a house for a family in need, or they imagine themselves teaching someone to read. They value letting their elected leaders know what they think of certain impending actions, or they want to help a family learn new ways of making good decisions.

But these interested and interesting people don't have any carpentry training. They haven't a clue how to teach an adult how to read. They have never been taught how to write a letter to their congressional representative or a letter to the editor. They do not know how to be part of a team which "adopts" a family. They truly want to help but are frozen in place because no one has offered them a way to learn the skills or knowledge they believe they need to be effective.

Training is essential. Members in your congregation may have expertise they are willing to share. Human service agencies or cooperative ministries may offer training in certain aspects of interacting with people in need. You can invite "experts" to lead a training event at your building or attend something offered by them elsewhere. Denominations have resource people who are available for advice or workshops. Conferences offer seminars that provide needed skills and attitude training. Help people learn what they need to know in order to love their neighbor.

Keep the Scale of Your Project Doable

We want to eliminate poverty in the world. We want to ensure that everyone who wants to pursue further education can do so. As admirable as these and many other visions are, they *may* be beyond what any one group can do. Everyone may feel paralyzed when the task feels so big. Where to begin?

Especially when beginning to work on a mission concern, start small. Begin with something doable. Those involved in the work will feel the thrill of success and be ready for the next step and then the next one. No one knows in the beginning how big the project might get.

A youth minister in a Presbyterian church in Columbia, South Carolina, decided the teenagers could collect dollar bills in big soup kettles on Super Bowl Sunday as people were leaving the worship services. The youth decided the money would be given to local organizations which addressed hunger issues in their community. Another church heard about the project and thought the "Soup" collection was a good idea. The idea grew and grew and became known as Souper Bowl Sunday which has collected millions of dollars for people who are hungry through its annual, nationwide event.

Find Small Things for People Who Cannot Otherwise Participate

Some people are deeply committed to reaching out to others. They truly see this as a faithful way to live. They simply do not have time. They are highly engaged raising a family or caring for ill and aging parents. They may be physically unable to prepare meals for people who are homebound. Other members may be in deep pain because of divorce, wayward children, dying loved ones, or loss of job or business so that they have no energy to reach out. They are depleted themselves.

Mission ministry teams can discover ways to engage people who want to serve within their limitations, whatever they may be. People who are housebound can be taught and encouraged to write letters to people who are lonely or to governmental officials. They can search the Internet for resources used by other groups in the country to "change the world." People who are caregivers for others can add an additional box of cereal to their grocery list for a food pantry which serves hungry people.

Suppose a donated box of cereal goes to a woman who has never had to ask for assistance before. She has recently been laid off, and her children are hungry. She is embarrassed even to have to ask. During the interview for a bag of food, she admits that she dropped out of school and the only work she's been able to get are dead-end jobs with no benefits and no future. The interviewer tells her about an employment program and an adult education program which can help her earn her GED. She checks out those programs.

During her process in the employment program, she admits that she has always dreamed of a career in the medical field. She learns that a class to train as a Certified Nurse Assistant is just beginning. She passes all the screening, gets accepted into the program, completes the training, and passes her state certification. She is hired in a full-time job with benefits. After a time she earns her Licensed Practical Nurse designation. She comes back to the food pantry with a big smile—and a box of cereal to help someone else.

The person who brought the seemingly insignificant box of cereal made a difference in the life of someone who was hurting.

Provide Support

Occasionally people are already involved in some type of ministry in the community. They feel as if their service is not embraced by their congregation. There is no formal "dedication and consecration" for their gifts of care and compassion; there is no one in their faith family they can talk with about their frustrations, joys, successes, and doubts; and they are given no formal way within their church fellowship to share their enthusiasm, passion, and commitment to this community ministry.

Because of this perceived lack of affirmation, these members might not fully trust the invitation to get involved in a project sponsored by the church. They have not received support in their own area of involvement and thus question how much support they would receive for this additional commitment.

On the other hand, a dedicated group within the congregation may want a long-term mission commitment. They are full of energy and plans. They have worked tirelessly to work out the details for a specific involvement on a community issue. After all their hard work, leadership of the congregation or the pastor does not endorse their taking this project forward. There is a danger they will withdraw from further involvement because of the feeling that "whatever we propose will get shot down." (Note: As enticing as it is to pout and quit caring beyond the church walls, this "no" may be simply God's way of indicating that the time is not yet right for proceeding. Continue to pray and consider how God is leading the group toward service to the community in Jesus' name.)

People need support to keep on doing the good they are doing.

No Matter the Reason

You will never have 100 percent of the members involved in service ministry. However, you can nurture the sense of call from Jesus to serve others by offering ways to be included in the caring ministries of the congregation, as well as by issuing challenges to the task. A person might not want to work on a Habitat house but would love baking a cake for the volunteers who are hammering. Someone who would not want to lead a mission trip to another community might love to create small gifts for people in homeless shelters.

Goethe said, "There is one elementary truth the ignorance of which kills countless ideas and splendid plans: the moment one definitely commits oneself, then Providence moves, too. All sorts of things occur to help one that never otherwise would have occurred … Whatever you can do or dream you can do, begin it. Boldness has genius, power and magic in it. Begin it now."

Caring for others is a God-given thing to do. No matter what—do it.

Questions to Consider

1. Where did you find yourself in these descriptions?

2. Are any of these descriptions accurate for people you know?

3. If you've tried to encourage people to get involved and they haven't, do you now have insights that might address their reluctance (either for yourself or for them)? Please explain.

4. What changes will you make in recruiting people for projects of service to others?

Exercise
Why I Am Afraid to Get Involved

A self-inventory of fears and concerns about getting involved can be helpful when you and church leaders are discerning how, when, and with whom to engage in direct ministries of service to others. You can use the following checklist and then discuss with each other what you learn.

Instructions: Check all that apply to you. If you are doing this exercise in a group, share your completed list with your group (as you are comfortable). Discuss ways to address these concerns individually and together. You can also commit to ways you will support each other.

The thing that frightens me about serving someone else is:

☐ Serving may take too much time.

☐ My serving may not be appreciated.

☐ I may get physically hurt.

☐ I may become too involved.

☐ Service may require more of me than I choose to give.

☐ I may not know anybody.

☐ Serving may show my ignorance, prejudices, fear, shyness, etc.

☐ I may see something about myself that I don't like.

☐ It may affect family relationships.

☐ It may cost me money.

☐ I may get conned.

☐ I may be emotionally hurt.

☐ It may make me seem weird to my friends.

☐ It may lead to the realization that it could be me.

☐ The people I'm serving may think I'm too little, too young, too old, too rich, too ignorant, etc.

Exercise Questions to Consider

1. Why did you check the statements you did?

2. How could you minimize these fears?

3. What would make it easier to get involved even if you are afraid?

Part Three:

Poverty: The Big Picture

Chapter Thirteen
Branching Out

*A*S WE BECOME MORE aware of poverty in our midst, many of us want to do something about it. In Part Three, we will look at poverty with wider lenses and deepen our understanding of how we can love our neighbor. We will consider some examples of how to confront issues which prolong poverty.

Levels of Poverty

Not only can we offer change to individuals or specific families, but we can also challenge cultural and systemic processes that cause or prolong poverty. We can be aware of the different levels of addressing poverty so that we value the person who ladles soup every Saturday as well as the agitator who seeks changes in minimum wage laws and delivery of health care, safe and affordable housing options, and access to transportation. We do not want to become complacent and close our eyes to the need for the other levels, nor do we want to become self-righteous by thinking that our way of addressing poverty is the only way.

1. Addressing the symptoms

The first level of working with poverty deals with the symptoms. If someone is hungry, we provide a soup kitchen, a bag of food, or a food voucher. If someone needs a home, we provide a bed at night and a mailing address during the day. If someone needs clothing, we offer a clothes closet for choosing an outfit. We don't dwell on why the need exists. We deal with the immediate need.

2. Helping a specific household or group of people overcome barriers to self sufficiency

The second level of working with poverty addresses the reasons the individual needs food or a bed. Maybe the person needs more job training or help in furthering her education. Maybe he needs some counseling or mentoring. We help the family or individual solve the issues that resulted in need. We attempt to strengthen skills and improve the situation of the family so they no longer need soup kitchens, night shelter beds, or rent assistance.

3. Confronting the systems that result in poverty

The third level asks, "What is going on in our community and in our world that a person does not earn enough money to adequately care for one's family even though one is working at least forty hours a week? Why can't a family move into a house that is safe and decent and, although modest, affordable for them?" The third level addresses the problems within the culture that directly influence poverty in one's community. We work as advocates to change society's existing systems of values, priorities, and focus.

Each level is important. *If* we as a society address *only one* of them—no matter which one—we will cause or continue extreme suffering for a significant group of our neighbors.

We will now consider one third-level issue: the availability and affordability of housing for people with extremely low income.

Is the Need Housing or Income? [14]

The answer is simple: "YES!"

Housing for all residents depends *both* on an adequate supply of low-cost housing *and* on enough income to make that housing affordable.

Values may be in conflict when a neighborhood or area is being considered for redevelopment. Developers want to clear blight. They will bring new homes, opportunities, and businesses. They will increase the tax base. Their changes within the neighborhood will reduce crime. Roads will now be wide enough for public service vehicles to collect trash, provide fire and police protection, and transport medical emergencies. There will be sidewalks, traffic lights, stop signs, and speed bumps. The community will be safer. Who could argue with all these benefits?

However, there are equally valid concerns for caution about how neighborhood changes happen. Legitimate businesses which remained in the community through its bleak years may get pushed out. Taxes will rise so that longtime residents can no longer afford to live in the neighborhood. Renters who need the existing cheap housing may wonder where they can move. Current residents say, "This is my home. I was born here. My children were born here." An elderly widow may have inherited the house and wish to remain in familiar surroundings. Another resident hears promises for one of the new houses but knows he may not qualify because of poor credit or inadequate work history. People who have lived in the neighborhood for years, of course, want reduced crime, more efficient trash removal, improved government services, and better traffic flow. *Additionally*, they want the community to be the way it *used* to be before everyone who had the resources to move out left the neighborhood.

The values on both sides of this desire to improve the community are equally valid. We need to hear the belief of some residents that developers do not have their welfare at heart. We need to attend to the perception that "I don't have any power or any options like rich folks do." We need to hear the voices of the people who are most directly affected—positively as well as negatively—when "outsiders" come to improve the area.

There are basic questions about whether the issue is income to afford housing or the availability of housing.

A minimum-wage worker (at the time of this writing minimum is $5.85 an hour) can afford monthly rent of no more than $304. Places renting for this amount may have no appliances or heat source. Public housing authorities may have long waiting lists for current apartments and closed application processes for housing vouchers because of similarly long waiting lists.

The housing wage needed in a community varies by community. (Note: The definition of housing wage is the amount a full-time worker must earn per hour to afford a two-bedroom unit at the area's fair market rate. [40 hours a week, 52 weeks a year, 30% of income for a two-bedroom unit at fair market rate.] Information about your state or county can be found at the Web site of the National Low Income Housing Coalition.)

There are gaps in availability of housing. Some communities are better than others. For example, according to the National Low Income Housing Coalition in 2004, there were only 60 affordable and available rental units for every 100 extremely low-income households in South Carolina. (Note: Extremely low income is defined as 30% or less of the area median income.)

Many communities have gaps in the number of emergency shelter beds needed, especially for families or individuals suffering from addiction or other diseases. There are often gaps in housing for people moving from homelessness to permanent housing and for people in job skills training, substance abuse rehabilitation, or mental health treatment programs. Gaps exist for people who need permanent housing with associated support services—people with disabilities or people living with mental illness or HIV/AIDS. Affordable rental housing is needed.

Home-ownership training and education continue to be important. We have seen the danger of enticing mortgage products that attracted many low-income, less-educated, and younger consumers. People who have rented need training in home ownership. They need to learn how to take care of their house and to fulfill all the related financial obligations. They need to be reminded that there is no longer a landlord to take care of repairs. Fixing what is broken is now their responsibility.

Housing solutions require many approaches. We as people of faith can own up to a moral obligation to make sure all residents have affordable housing available to them. Some of the ways we can be advocates are:

Call for fair and just zoning and density laws.

Commit funds to help nonprofit housing developers create new homes.

Hold our elected officials accountable for providing adequate housing for all residents.

Protect low income homeowners who are caught in escalating taxes and insurance needs in gentrifying neighborhoods.

Advocate for fair and just wages for people who work hard and still cannot provide for their families.

Develop single-room homes, housing with support services, rental apartments, and homes for purchase.

Highlight the disconnect between what workers earn and what housing costs. For example, in Greenville County, South Carolina, elementary school teachers, police officers, licensed practical nurses, and retail salespersons cannot afford the average purchase price of a home. [15]

Congregations are very good at dealing with poverty at the first level, where they address the symptoms. Many churches have clothes closets, soup kitchens, or food pantries. They support night shelters or at times provide overnight shelter in their own facilities. Other congregations move to the second level, helping someone grow toward self-sufficiency, when they establish a program to work with specific families or provide adult education classes. Fewer congregations choose to work on the third level, confronting the systems leading to poverty.

Let's continue with the issue of housing as a third-level poverty concern. Communities can choose to address the issues of income and availability. Isn't that what a just and committed community does? However, sometimes people need to be convinced that housing is an issue in their community. They must see before they will become motivated to do something.

An effective way to engage people in helping change your community is to take them on a tour of blighted areas—a poverty tour. Show them the "other side" of your community. Point out how close poor neighborhoods are to areas they pass through regularly. Help open their eyes to parts of your city or county that even longtime residents may not know exist.

Touring Blighted Areas

Developing a poverty tour takes some time and research, but the payoffs for helping others see with their eyes, smell with their noses, and feel in their gut are worth the initial investment of time. Once people know that you will take them out to learn, you will have many opportunities to share this important experience.

Just a note about the tour: When you are ready to lead a tour, some may suggest that the tour has the feel of going through a "zoo," and they are embarrassed. Listen empathetically and affirm their feelings. Then offer the alternative understanding that until people see what is in their own community, they will feel no compulsion to do anything about it. Showing a PowerPoint presentation of these neighborhoods does not have the same in-your-gut impact as seeing them with one's own eyes. Hiding behind our embarrassment does not help us become motivated to change the conditions in which our neighbors are forced to live.

Identify Neighborhoods and Areas to Visit

The first step in developing a poverty tour is to identify the neighborhoods and areas you will include. Look for neighborhoods known to have high concentrations of poverty. You can discover them in several ways:

1. Ask participants in programs for people with limited resources where those neighborhoods are.
2. Look at tax records for properties with low tax base. Look at the ratio of home ownership to rental.
3. Ask city officials which neighborhoods are targeted for redevelopment and how to get to those areas.
4. Ask public and/or affordable housing professionals where low-income neighborhoods are.
5. Ask teachers, social workers, and health-care professionals who do home visits.

6. Ask people who work with homeless people where homeless people might be staying.
7. *The best way!* Get in your car, drive around. Usually, if you move two or three blocks off main thoroughfares, you'll be able to tell you are in an area with high concentrations of poverty. Explore your own community with new eyes.

Research the Neighborhood's History

The second step is to research the history of the neighborhoods included in your tour. Were they developed as areas for low-income households? If not, what happened that they became low-income neighborhoods? Who abandoned the neighborhoods?

You can find some of this information by talking with people who are local history buffs—professors, historic preservationists, genealogists, etc. If you're lucky, your local or state university library will have books or documents that tell the area's history. There are always residents who have been in the area for years, if not generations, who will share their memories and experiences.

Share this information as appropriate.

You may also think about what policies, ordinances, and laws maintain the existence of neighborhoods that can only be described as blighted. You might offer the premise that laws are made by people to protect the people who make the laws. For example, the old Jim Crow laws in the South which separated white people from black people were made by ... white people. Those laws certainly did not benefit black people. However, significant numbers of white people felt safer and more comfortable with those laws than without them. As you tour, discuss how laws benefit those who make the laws and hurt, intentionally or inadvertently, those who do not have such power.

Find out what the units rent for in the neighborhoods you are touring. You can do this by calling landlords whose signs are posted on the buildings or by calling housing counselors in your area.

The issue of slumlords might need some research. As you drive people through neighborhoods, tour participants may begin blaming the owners of the rental properties for the bad conditions of the houses. Certainly some landlords ignore the condition of their housing and charge high rents. They add to the victimization of residents in the community by taking money and providing bare-bones services. If you look on the tax rolls to discover who owns the properties, you may be horrified at some of the names you discover. You may discover that one of these landlords is someone you play golf with—or who sits on your pew at church!

Categorizing all low-rent landlords as slumlords may not do justice to the entire picture, however. Some owners really do want to maintain their property. They may put kitchen appliances in the unit—only to have them stolen. After two or three thefts, the owner quits trying to provide a refrigerator or a stove. At other times, replacing a furnace might necessitate raising the rent to cover the costs of repairs in addition to the landlord's taxes and insurance.

A property owner may prefer to continue renting to the current tenant at the current affordable rate rather than do needed repairs. If he fixed everything, he would have to increase the rent to cover expenses. The longtime tenant would be forced out.

Sometimes the landlord might prefer to tear down an existing unit and build a new one, but current building codes regarding density would require that two units on contiguous lots be torn down to accommodate the *one* replacement unit. Therefore, one more housing unit would be lost. Sometimes the cost of repairs would price the unit totally out of the range for the neighborhood.

The issue of low-income rental property has a lot of gray areas about it. As one landlord who is committed to justice said, "Someone has to provide this housing. I choose to do it, but I must also make some money to be able to do it. I am not a charity." Another landlord quipped, "Bad housing is better than no housing or better than living in a car." This last comment is certainly open to discussion. Simply blaming the landlords does not get to a deeper understanding of how this kind of housing happened in the first place and what regulations hinder major improvements.

Identify Points to Highlight on the Tour

The third step is to identify the points you wish to highlight on the tour. If you discover paths into wooded areas or bamboo thickets, look carefully for evidence of human habitation. For example, do you see clothing, cans, bottles, roofs made of cardboard or tarpaulins, or similar items? You might also look for seeming trash under shrubs near buildings. Look high under bridges. Do you see evidence of human habitation—sleeping bags, clothing, cans, etc.?

If you see satellite dishes outside apartments or buildings where poor people live, help the tour participants understand that people may have satellite dishes on their apartments for one of the following reasons: (1) Entertainment is very important to people of low income. (2) Immigrants, especially from Spanish-speaking countries, can keep up with news from home by watching programs in their own languages.

Look at the churches in the communities. Is there a significant number? What denominations are there? Does the number of churches undergird or dispel the notion that people who are poor are not religious?

If you find houses that are dilapidated but have very nice cars parked in front, offer the understanding that it is *much* easier to get a car loan than a house loan. Most people might not know where someone lives, but they will notice the car she drives to work, to visit relatives and friends, or to attend church. People need reliable cars to get to and from work and to take children to the doctor.

If some houses have tiny rooms attached to the rear, these are probably bathrooms added when government ordinance discontinued outdoor plumbing. Notice the neighborhoods that have such add-ons. In some communities the ordinance required that city water be run *to* the house, not *into* the house! The people living there might not have had the resources to connect the water. The landlord might not have chosen to attach the water. Many of the add-on bathrooms had only a toilet and a sink. They may or may not have been connected to the water or sewer system. A number of these connected bathrooms originally had a door opening to the outside rather than into the house.

If you see wooden pallets piled in a yard, assume that this is firewood. Some locales do not require landlords to furnish heat. The ordinance might read, "If the unit has a heat source, it must be functional." No heat means the residents must heat with wood in a fireplace (Note: wooden pallets are made from pine treated with creosote and liable to cause chimney fires), or the family heats with kerosene, which leaves a distinctive odor on their clothing.

Houses that are boarded up may have people living in them, even though there is no electricity or water. Notice whether the boards covering doorways are actually nailed up or are simply leaning on the door. Loose boards at a window allow access inside. Occasionally the windows will be boarded up, and the door will be standing wide open. Abandoned buildings often provide shelter for people who have nowhere else to go.

Pay attention to what is different about the low-wealth neighborhoods. In addition to the houses being small, old, and in disrepair, they may lack sidewalks, gutters, lighting, or driveways. Trash may be piled on the sides of the street. Roads may be extremely narrow. You may see wooden pallets for firewood piled up. Help people on the tour notice these things. You may ask, "What is missing from this neighborhood?" and let them see for themselves the discrepancies between where they live and where people who are poor and who have limited options are living.

Ask, "Does this neighborhood feel safe for children? Why or why not? What are the implications for the future for children raised in the conditions you've observed on this tour?"

Engage Your Tour Participants

The fourth step is to engage your tour participants so they can be inspired to do something with what they have seen. Remind your tour participants that the current residents in the neighborhoods you are touring did not cause these neighborhoods to be in the conditions they are. *The circumstances that resulted in the now-obvious blight were often beyond their control.* People with decision-making power in the past helped create these neighborhoods—for good or ill. Infrequent garbage collection leads to more and more garbage being dumped. Residents' lack of raise-hell power to make their voices and complaints heard can limit public vision and appropriate improvements.

When you have completed the tour, offer suggestions for ways to get involved in changing the community. Some ideas are:

1. Write letters to your officials.

2. Get involved with community groups that are trying to make a difference.
3. Encourage others to go on the tour.
4. Suggest that their faith community develop a presence in the community.
5. Go to the National Low Income Housing Coalition's Web site (www.nlich.org) and find out information specific to your county. Their *Out of Reach* section is full of vital information about any area in the country.

Pay Attention to Safety Issues

One final step is always to pay attention to safety issues. Keep doors locked. Know places where it is safe to stop your tour vehicle and those where it is not. Know where people can safely get out of the vehicle to walk around and where they should not. Taking private cars is not as safe as taking a vehicle clearly marked as belonging to an agency or a congregation. Driving too slowly in a personal car looks more like you are seeking a drug buy and less like an educational tour. Waving at residents you encounter helps everyone know that you mean no harm.

These precautions are important. However, when you become known in the affected communities as someone who cares and who wants to make a difference, people will actually wave to you as you drive by. You must always remember that these neglected neighborhoods attract people with mental-health issues, addicts, or those involved in criminal activity. These are the same folks the longtime residents would like removed from their communities. They do not want to live close to these dangers any more than you or I would.

This is one example of how to develop a poverty tour. There may be helping organizations, work situations, or ecological issues that you want to include. The length and scope of the tour are limited only by your own creativity and interests. When people have an opportunity to see with their own eyes, this is a powerful incentive for them to become involved in loving their neighbors in wiser and more compassionate ways.

After you conduct a poverty tour, members of your congregation may decide they are ready to address housing issues in your community. They may begin to question zoning and density laws. They can wonder how contracts are made and who gets them. They may ask, "Who is in charge here? Who is responsible for this blight? What can we do?"

Know that when you decide to confront long-standing systems that allow and even encourage poverty, you likely will take on issues without quick solutions. Taking on the status quo will not provide the immediate affirmation you get by giving someone a bag of food. Deciding to challenge how community decisions are made takes much more time and energy than helping one family learn how to hold a job, manage their money, and educate themselves and their children.

All three levels of addressing poverty are essential. If someone is bleeding, we must put on a bandage. If someone continues to need bandages, we can work with him or her to avoid doing whatever leads to the need for bandages. At some point, we may wonder, "What is going on so that people keep getting cut? How can we change that?"

You can soothe the pain caused by the symptoms of poverty by offering food, a shelter, bed, or clothing. You can help a family overcome specific issues in their own situation that are keeping them in poverty. You can challenge decisions that prolong poverty. All these approaches are important. Which way(s) will you choose to love your neighbor?

Questions to consider

1. Which level of working with poverty are you most passionate about? Why?

2. Which level of working with poverty is the easiest for you to consider doing? Why?

3. Which level of poverty work is the most difficult for you to consider doing? Why?

4. Go to www.nlihc.org, and click on "Out of Reach" to discover the cost of rental housing and the required housing wage in your area. Is the average hourly wage in your community close to the housing wage needed? If not, do you want to do something about that? Why, or why not?

5. Do you know where low-cost rental housing is in your community? If so, how would you describe that housing?

6. How much substandard housing is in your community? How do you feel about the amount?

7. Does anyone in your community offer a tour of blighted areas? If the answer is no, who might be willing to design and offer a poverty tour?

Chapter Fourteen
Justice and Charity Are Not the Same

*P*EOPLE SOMETIMES USE THE terms "justice" and "charity" to mean the same thing. These terms are not synonymous. In this chapter we will look at the differences between the two concepts. We will delve into the balance required for doing justice. We will consider how our view of economics governs how we perceive measures to confront poverty and the issues it creates.

Charity

Charity comes from a position of wanting to "do good." Charity allows us to help from a position of wealth, strength, or correctness. When we offer charity, we decide what, when, how, and to whom we will give. It allows us to share something with someone, but we do not have to connect with him or her in any way.

We can take our used clothes to a helping agency and know that the clothes will be given to someone in need. We don't have to worry about the fit of the coat or even the condition of the coat we donate. We assume that if someone is cold, any old coat will do. We *never* have to move from our comfort or security to offer charity to someone. We can help and not be touched in any kind of deep, spiritual way. We give to meet a specific need—food, clothing, rent money, homes, etc. From a charity standpoint, we do not question why the person needs our used coat, our bag of groceries, or our financial gift. We simply meet the immediate need.

Justice

Justice, on the other hand, asks why the person cannot afford to purchase his or her own coat. What is going on within the family so they cannot afford their rent? Justice can go even further by asking risky questions such as "Why does our community allow employers to pay service workers so poorly that they cannot afford to feed their families, provide adequate shelter, or clothe their children?" "What is it about our community that makes it difficult for people who truly want to work to be able to work? Is it lack of transportation? Is it lack of access to health care?" You may think of other questions.

In understanding the justice Jesus called for, we want for others what we want for ourselves, and we work to make that happen. Jesus' pronouncement of the two most important commandments helps us move from charity to justice. He said: "You shall love the Lord your God with all your heart, and with all your soul, and with all your mind, and with all your strength.... You shall love your neighbor as yourself" (see Mark 12:28–34). Wanting for our neighbor exactly what we want for ourselves defines justice. (Note: See Chapter 2 for further discussion.)

A Room Full of Masks

I have a fantasy that may help expand our understanding of justice. It goes like this. Sometimes I wish there were a room for people to visit. This room is filled with different masks. Some masks are faces of old people. One visage looks like the model for an ad for senior citizens' cruises. Another is lined and well-worn. One's hair is well-coiffed. Another's is frizzy and straggly.

There are masks of men's faces, women's faces, children's faces. Masks are European, African, Asian, Native American, and Middle Eastern. One group of masks are faces of people who are homeless or very poor. Another group has faces showing the benefits of money, good nutrition, and appropriate cosmetics.

There are masks for Presbyterians, Baha'is, Baptists, Pentecostals, Catholics, New Agers, Unitarians, Mormons, Moslems, Methodists,

Hindus, and all other faiths. There would be masks for straights and gays, for educated and uneducated, rich, poor, loved, and battered.

There are hundreds of masks in this room.

Every one of us is required to go into the room and put on whatever mask the attendant gives to us. The choice is the attendant's, not ours. For the next thirty days, we become whoever our mask tells us we are.

If we had to feel the feelings of someone else or live the realities of another person for an entire month, how would our world be different?

This is doing justice.

The Shalom Balance of Justice

A nonprofit dedicated its annual meeting to two men who had died the previous year. Fred was a faithful volunteer and the other, Willie, a homeless man, a recipient of services. One was someone we would all admire, and the other was someone we might try to avoid. One was every parent's dream and the other every parent's worst fear. Both men were significant parts of the community. Both men were part of the nonprofit's life.

As I thought about these two, I kept seeing in my mind's eye those scales that sat on the counters of the old-time grocery stores. You know the ones. They work like a seesaw. When the balance is correct, the pans are level with each other. When one side gets more weight on it than the other, the scales are tipped. As I thought about those scales, the word *shalom* came to mind. (Note: See Chapter 4 for earlier discussion about *shalom*.)

Shalom is a biblical word and is still in use today. Today the word *shalom* is often translated as "peace." When people say "peace," they often mean an absence of conflict or tension such as when we teach children to stop fighting *now* and to say: "I'm sorry." The children may grit their teeth and spit out, "I'm sorry," and stop the obvious scuffling, but is there true peace? I don't know. Some of us think of peace as a state of inertia as when we sit on a porch and rock and rock and rock and just let our minds float. We can think, "How peaceful." *Or* peace might mean the cessation of responsibility, as when we tell our spouse, "Just let me be. Don't keep telling me I need to—whatever."

On the other hand, the deeper meaning of *shalom* has a connotation of wholeness, a relationship of communion, a state of harmonious equilibrium, and relationships that are whole between individuals themselves, between them and God, and between themselves and nature. *Shalom* carries the picture of those balanced scales, where no one is higher or lower than any other. Everyone has whatever it takes to be healthy and secure. The balance of *shalom* is where we find justice and a healthy community.

Making the *shalom* kind of peace means that we confront the veneers of doing good in the name of making money. For example, some companies today are using the word "green" to make themselves appear more eco-friendly when, in fact, they have altered none of their polluting or wasteful processes.

Making *shalom* peace means that we provide whatever is necessary for people to be able to live full, productive, and enriched lives.

Making *shalom* peace means we confront stereotypes being promulgated.

Making *shalom* peace means we say we do not agree with how decision makers are choosing in favor of people with power rather for people without power.

Making *shalom* peace means we look at the scales, study where the balance is off, and work to bring balance back.

Looking for Shalom Balance

When I drive through blighted neighborhoods in our area, I am acutely aware of the lack of balance in our community. Those neighborhoods have no sidewalks, no gutters or curbs, and sporadic trash pickup. They lack safe places for children to play. As a resident of another downtown neighborhood, I have sidewalks, gutters and curbs, weekly trash pickup, and a park within one block of my house. When I tour these poverty-ridden neighborhoods with a group, we visually see the lack of balance between the neighborhoods we are riding through and the neighborhoods where many of us live.

When we begin to notice the lack of balance in our community or when we decide we want to "do something" to help other people, we get a group of people together and plan for changes. We meet with appropriate government officials, we write letters, we raise money, we organize people for work crews, and we challenge the beliefs that "this is the way it's always been and the way it will always be." If you were not committed to improving life for your neighbors, you would not be reading this book, would you? You and I care. We want others to enjoy the benefits and opportunities we enjoy. We work hard for justice and mercy.

Becoming Aware of the Underbelly of Doing Good

Sometimes, in our efforts to help, we actually hurt people. I'll share just a few examples of how people tried to do the right thing and in the process caused pain to others. They truly and deeply helped some people but inadvertently hurt others—sometimes significantly.

Two housing complexes owned by the local public housing authority had a total of 350 rental units which charged rents of 30 percent of tenants' household incomes. People who had no income could live there as well as those who could easily pay $400 or more per month. Admittedly, the apartments were bad. They needed renovation, but the renovations still would not have brought them to code. They concentrated poverty with all the problems that come with it … drugs, bugs, guns, and violence.

The housing authority received a grant that allowed them to tear down all the apartments. The grant also assisted residents in moving elsewhere. Gorgeous and precious brand new homes are available on the same site today. The subsidies for purchase keep the prices around $100,000 more or less. The people who are lucky enough to purchase a home there are truly blessed. I am thrilled for them to live in an award-winning neighborhood and for them to have the opportunities that home ownership provides for them.

But guess how many rental units are there now? Remember there were once 350. Would you guess 200? 100? No. There are 35 units, and they are for senior citizens. In doing good … *good* … for certain folks, the community lost 315 units of subsidized rental housing. That's 315 families who may have found even better housing than the apartments, but it may also be 315 families who now live in places where we wouldn't want our dogs to live. On one side of the scales of *shalom* balance, families who may never have had the opportunity to own a house now live in their own home. On the other side of the balance, families who need really inexpensive housing have more and more difficulty finding it.

Another example: A new construction site is across the street from my office. Young urban professionals are scooping up the houses being built in the three city blocks of the developing area. The homes are attractive, with a lot of green space included in the planning. They are two blocks from a major tourist attraction. A two-story brick building under construction immediately across the street will have condos and offices and retail space.

The Relax Inn Motel was on that site several years ago. Then, you could get anything illegal at the Relax Inn. Residents of the neighborhood as well as city planners wanted the motel to be gone. No one could argue that the illegal activities were a true nuisance and menace. However, the motel was also home to a significant number of people. For a weekly fee, they had heat, water, air-conditioning, and television. Nowhere else could they live so cheaply with amenities— such as they were. Some people had lived at the Relax Inn for years ... nine years, thirteen years.

When it came time to tear down the motel, there was a big celebration with balloons and sparkling juice served in champagne flutes on the motel side of the street. On our side of the street people had tears in their eyes because their home was being torn down. Our staff had helped relocate those we could, but we could not find housing for everyone. On one side of the scales of *shalom* balance, removing a blight on the community was smart and the right thing to do. On the other side of the balance, a number of people lost their homes with no other options immediately available to them.

Another illustration: The renter wage in Greenville County, South Carolina, needs to be $11.06 an hour. That's what it takes to spend 30 percent of your household income for renting a two-bedroom apartment at the fair market rate of $623. With the minimum wage currently at $5.85 an hour, the most a minimum wage worker can afford at 30 percent of income is an apartment that rents for $304. An apartment renting that cheaply may not have a heat source, and it may not have appliances in the kitchen.

Many of us are determined advocates for paying people fair wages so that, when they work hard and long, they can adequately take care of their families. We argue that if we want people to be able to be responsible, we have to pay them just wages. However, many companies might not be able to afford paying $11.06 an hour and so would be forced to eliminate jobs. Earning less than $11.06 an hour is better than earning no money at all. Some companies might have to raise the prices on the goods they produce, which could mean fewer goods purchased. On one side of the scales of *shalom* balance, some people would finally be earning an income that allows them to be adequate providers for their families. On the other side of the scale, some people might have no work at all.

Am I saying that we are not to try to change our world for the betterment of all our citizens because of the downsides? *No way*. We are compelled to try to do everything we can to help our neighbors. We are to reach out to Willie, to the people who are on the fringes of our society. Many of us can imagine no other way of living than to reach out to people around us. Our service to others defines our very being, just as Fred's volunteer commitment defined him. We are called in various ways to engage ourselves and our neighbors to create communities of *shalom* where everyone has the opportunity to become the person he or she was created to be from birth until now.

Being Mindful of Balancing the Scale

What I *am* saying is that we must pay attention to the *shalom* scale when we propose to solve a problem in our community. When we want to tear down horrid apartments, will we address the need that those dwellings were fulfilling, the need for very inexpensive housing? When we tear down crime-infested motels that function as single-room rental units, will we address that need? When we plan a new thing, will we be mindful of the downsides of our plan and try to reduce the pain to those most deeply affected by the old?

At a recent staff meeting, we learned of a landlord who does not check references and rents to people who have criminal backgrounds. He is providing housing to people who literally have no other option than the street. However, he charges for everything. Not only does a tenant pay rent for the room, he rents the bed in which he sleeps. He rents the television. He pays an extra $25 a month to use the handicapped ramp for his wheelchair. Our first response as a staff was "We need to close this landlord down. How dare he take the entire $625 disability check for our program participant!"

Then a staff member cautioned us with a *shalom* voice. "Hey, wait a minute. We can't go after him until we have a solution for those folks who live in his properties because they literally have no place else to go." This then becomes the plan: Find options for those most vulnerable folks before going after the obvious wrong that needs to be confronted.

Many of us love to be catalysts in our community to bring about good things for those on the bottom of the economic ladder. Our challenge is to fully think through all the issues of our plans. It's easy to dwell on thoughts about those who will benefit by what we are about. It's harder to consider those who may be hurt by our actions.

Will some folks be hurt or left out as a result of what we do? Of course. Some people will get mad and try to thwart us simply because we want to change the system. At times our work means that some people will not continue to benefit too much at the expense of those who benefit too little. That ticks some people off. Sometimes we have to choose which group of folks we want to help because we cannot help everyone. Sometimes our best efforts are very painful for some of our neighbors.

Accepting the Challenge

My challenge to us all is:

> Think about those who will be hurt by our so-called improvements.
> Talk seriously with those who will be affected.
> Alter our plans to accommodate more of the needs of those affected when possible.
> Try to see life through the eyes of the people who need our services.
> Listen to our decisions with the heart of a dedicated volunteer.
> Remember *shalom* and its scales of balance.

When we work to balance the *shalom* scales for justice, we will improve the quality of life for people. We will become change agents for all of us, not just for some of us. We can work to create justice in our communities. We can strive to live out our faith as Jesus taught through his own life and teaching.

Even so, we will still be influenced by our understanding of the politics of economics. In other words, we will think about solving problems of poverty based on what we think about money: how one gets it, what one does with it, and what to do with people who don't have it.

Economic Theories Affect Our Lives

Our perception of economic theory governs how we transact business or what we think about the national trends of economic development. Our understanding of economic theory affects how we function in our personal financial lives and determines the solutions we might develop for "improving" people who are not economically healthy.

The following is a very simple description (in other words, not from an economist's point of view) of three theories of economics. The source for these theories was a study developed by the Evangelical Lutheran Church in America (ELCA) in conjunction with its social statement entitled *Give Us This Day Our Daily Bread: Sufficient, Sustainable Livelihood for All.* [16] Even if the theories are not articulated in a sophisticated way, they help us understand why we might believe our approach is the correct one to use for helping people.

Theory A

Markets are impersonal, unbiased means through which those who seek to make a profit produce efficiently to meet the desires of customers. The goal is to do as well as or better than competitors, or else be driven out of the market by losses. Markets are efficient, self-regulating, and tend to employ all productive resources. The flexibility of the prices of goods and services, credit (interest rates), and labor (wages and salaries) assure that the products most

desired by consumers will be produced through
the least costly means. The process of production
generates incomes for workers and for those who
provide other resources (land, financial capital,
management skills) that enable them to buy the
products they most desire. If some producers
gain market power and drive competitors out of
business, their excessive profits will soon attract new
competitors into the market. Government should
allow these dynamics of the market system as free a
reign as possible, and limit its role to protecting life
and property and enforcing contracts. [17]

How Theory A Addresses Poverty

Since the free market allows anyone to have the American dream
if they want it badly enough and work hard enough, people in need
should be helped only through voluntary efforts of individuals and
charities. Poverty is a poor person's own fault. If the poor are not
succeeding, they are to blame. They are lazy or made bad decisions
and deserve what they get.

The Downside of Theory A

There is no such thing as the free market anymore. Huge
government subsidies have taken that away. When farmers are paid not
to plant crops or are guaranteed a certain price, when companies are
provided tax incentives or are given land for building their facilities,
then the market is not truly free. Regulations and laws devised to
protect certain segments of the economy eliminate the possibility of
making it solely through one's efforts.

Theory B

A market system has important strengths, but it
also has shortcomings. Some people, including
children, the disabled, and the frail elderly, cannot
earn an adequate income through their own labor.
Others who are willing and able to work cannot

find employment because they lack the necessary education or skills. They cannot work because of a declining economy. When a market is dominated by one or a very few buyers or sellers, they set high prices and take excessive profits. Top management personnel and corporate shareholders receive ever higher incomes, while many others find their real incomes declining. Advertising continually creates desires for new goods and services. [18]

How Theory B Addresses Poverty

Vulnerable people in the population are unable to work through the free market. They are elderly, mentally challenged, disabled, or underage. They need government services and support to assist them, since they cannot benefit from opportunities to produce adequate income. Such programs might be subsidies, tax incentives, or training. Solutions might involve governmental policy and regulation in addition to private charitable organizations.

People are negatively affected by lack of education or employable skills. The community needs to provide opportunities for them to develop so that they can have jobs that pay decent wages. Folks should be taught also how to spend money on necessities, since advertising relentlessly encourages them to buy, buy, buy. The focus of helping programs is on the individual in need, whether through subsidies for those who truly cannot work or through training for those who lack skills.

The Downside of Theory B

Salaries for CEOs have increased several hundred percent while the minimum wage has fallen in purchasing power. Corporate profits rise while the average hourly wage stagnates. Thus even people with no disabilities may not be able to earn enough to care adequately for their families. People may work fifty to seventy hours a week at multiple part-time jobs and receive no benefits. They may have no insurance, no health care, or no time off (paid or not). They definitely are not lazy. They work hard and long and still do not have adequate resources for themselves and their families. Additionally, when vulnerable people depend solely on government programs and policies, they are always at risk of changes in political will that can result in programs being downsized or eliminated.

Theory C

> A market system is biased in favor of those with economic power, who tend to dominate or exploit those without much power. It is in the interest of employers that a significant portion of the labor force remain unemployed in order to keep wages down. Financial and natural resources ownership becomes concentrated in the hands of those who are able to control production decisions, prices, production levels, and buying and selling. Some firms grow to dominate entire sectors of the economy and exert significant political power. They are able to influence government, which becomes a tool through which they maintain their power and exercise control over other institutions of society. [19]

How Theory C Addresses Poverty

Solving problems related to excesses in power requires addressing major structural change. To prevent, for example, destruction of the environment by pollution requires intentional regulations against polluting activities, a change of mind-set about what is important for our world, and a reorientation of values. Therefore dealing with poverty requires systemic changes, new government regulations and policies, and private charitable activities.

Addressing poverty, then, might require changes in laws governing minimum wage, adequate health care for all citizens, and affordable and safe housing for everyone. Providing transportation so that people can get to jobs and appointments becomes essential. Addressing poverty demands that the human asset infrastructure changes so that people can benefit from wealth created through joint effort.

The Downside of Theory C

When people have concentrated power in addition to the resources to keep them in power, implementing changes in systems and values is extremely difficult. People with power will not see the need for relinquishing anything when the system works so well for them. The ultimate result of such a scenario is revolution.

When companies refuse to pay adequate wages because they can hire immigrants who are at the mercy of unjust employers, then salary scales are reduced for everyone. When companies move operations away from the United States, citizens with the desire, the skills, and the experience to work are left without employment to support their families. When medical services can bankrupt families, something is wrong. When a car is required to purchase a prescription or to go to work, things are out of balance in the society.

What Do We Do?

Each of these theories has strengths and weaknesses. We see evidence for each of them in our communities and our nation. Our challenge is to assess the needs we see, determine what those needs are, and then decide what the solution requires. We can ask:

Can we simply address the symptom as with Theory A?

Do we need to provide some minimal supports and add some legislative clout as with Theory B?

Do we need to change the heart and mind of a community and implement some radically new ways of living, working, and loving together as required by Theory C?

When we decide to view life through the lenses of people whose experiences are different from ours, we begin to yearn for justice. When we become change agents and not simply responders to existing needs, we move deeper and deeper into issues of poverty. We realize that solutions are complex. When we acknowledge that some of us are better suited to provide for immediate needs than to take on the powers of the world, we affirm the gifts and caring of us all. Together we thoughtfully explore and implement ways to love and help people in poverty.

We are called as people of faith to care for those who are vulnerable. We have considered many ideas about how to love our neighbors with wisdom and compassion. We have a variety of options that align with the variety of skills, gifts, and interests in our congregations and in our personal lives.

When I charge a congregation at the end of a worship service before giving the benediction, I say, "I charge you to be responsible and responsive wherever you are. Remember, because you have been here today, you can never be the same again." So now I charge you: Remember, because you have thoughtfully considered how to love your neighbor, you will never be the same again.

Questions to consider

1. What are examples of acts of charity and acts of justice within your congregation, your community, or your own life?

2. If you were given a mask, which mask would you enjoy receiving? Why?

3. If you were given a mask, which mask would you regret receiving? Why?

4. Do you have examples of a project that was "good" which also did "bad" to certain people?

5. Which economic theory most closely aligns with how you see the world? Why?

6. If you are part of a group trying to address poverty, how will the information in this chapter alter those solutions? Or will it?

Closing Exercise
A Creed for Helping Others [20]

I will not agree to help you go off the edge.

I will not agree to help you become a robotized normal and adjusted person.

I will not help you stay and wallow in the cesspool of your own making.

I will help you grow and become more productive, by your definition.

I will help you become more autonomous, more loving of yourself, more enthusiastic, and freer to continue becoming the authority of your own life.

I cannot give you your dreams. I cannot "fix you." I simply cannot.

I cannot make you grow or grow for you. You must do that for yourself.

I cannot take away your loneliness or pain.

I will not sense your world for you, evaluate your world for you, or tell you what is best for you in your world. Your world is yours, not mine.

I cannot convince you to choose the scary uncertainty of growing over the safe misery of not growing.

I want to be with you and respect you, but I will not if you are not choosing to grow.

When I begin to care for you out of pity or when I begin to lose trust in you, then I am not good for you. You are not good for me.

My helping you is conditional! I will be with you, and I will hang in there with you as long as I continue to get even the slightest hints that you are still trying to grow.

If you can accept all of this, then perhaps we can help each other.

Afterword

Helping others with wisdom and compassion can be immensely rewarding. Helping others when we feel as if we do not know what we're doing can be immensely frustrating. Planning ahead for some of the situations, feelings, obstacles, and successes which may happen increases the satisfaction for both the person offering assistance and the one receiving assistance. When we build relationships with others who can benefit from our assistance, their lives *and* ours are enriched beyond anything we can imagine. We all want to help. We want to love our neighbor in thoughtful, wise, and compassionate ways.

Notes

Introduction

1. Josh Shaffer, "Young Man Started from 'Scratch,' Learned Some Priceless Lessons," Greenville News, Greenville, SC, November 18, 2007.

Chapter Two: Loving Totally

2. Connie Rouse, "The Homecoming Triumph," story appearing originally in the South Carolina United Methodist Advocate (n.d.), used with permission.

Chapter Three: Walking the Way?

3. Anna Bartlett Warner, 1859 and William Batchelor Bradbury, 1861, "Jesus Loves Me!" The Presbyterian Hymnal (Westminster: John Knox Press, 1990), 304.

4. Shirley Guthrie, Always Being Reformed; Faith for a Fragmented World (Louisville, KY: Westminster Press, 1996), 70. Emphasis in original.

5. Presbyterian Church USA, 210th General Assembly, 1998.

6. Bennett Sims, newsletter quote, undated.

7. Original source of poem is unknown.

Chapter Four: Requirements of Faith

8. Marcus Borg, The Heart of Christianity (San Francisco, CA: HarperCollins, 2003), 127.

Chapter Five: Poverty in the Bible

9. The scriptures listed and questions to consider were adapted slightly from Nancy A. Carter, "Study Session Two," Keeping Covenant with the Poor (New York: Friendship Press, Inc., 1988), 7.

Chapter Six: When Someone in Need Approaches You

10. Adapted and used with permission. Originally appeared as an opinion piece by Beth Lindsay Templeton in the Greenville News, Greenville, SC, November 9, 2006.

Chapter Seven: Helping Others: Servant or Sucker?

11. Ruby Payne, Framework for Understanding Poverty (Highlands, TX: aha! Process, Inc., 1996).

12. Dreier, Peter, "Will President Bush Reform the Mansion Subsidy?" ShelterForce, Nov./Dec., 2005, www.nhi.org.

13. Agency ABC Application was adapted from ABS Instructor Training Manual (Whitfield, Parker, and Childress, 1992).

Chapter Thirteen: Branching Out

14. Adapted and used with permission. Originally appeared as an opinion piece by Beth Lindsay Templeton in the Greenville News, Greenville, SC, November 17, 2004.

15. Center for Housing Policy, "Paycheck to Paycheck," Web site search, Feb. 26, 2008.

Chapter Fourteen: Justice and Charity Are Not the Same

16. *Evangelical Lutheran Church In America (ELCA), Give Us This Day Our Daily Bread: Sufficient, Sustainable Livelihood for All, produced by the Department of Studies of the Division for Church in Society, 1999. 9–10.*

17. *ELCA materials, 1999.*

18. *ELCA materials, 1999.*

19. *ELCA materials, 1999.*

20. *"A Creed for Helping Others" was adapted from an unknown source.*